The series editors:

Adrian Beard is Head of English at Gosforth High School, Newcastle upon Tyne, and a chief examiner for A-Level English Literature. He has written and lectured extensively on the subjects of literature and language. His publications include *Texts and Contexts* (Routledge).

Angela Goddard is Senior Lecturer in Language at the Centre for Human Communication, Manchester Metropolitan University, and was Chief Moderator for English Language A-Level Project Research for the Northern Examination and Assessment Board (NEAB) from 1983 to 1995. She is now chair of examiners for A-Level English Language. Her publications include *Researching Language* (second edition; Heinemann, 2000).

Core textbook:
Working with Texts: A core introduction to language analysis
(second edition; 2001)
Ronald Carter, Angela Goddard, Danuta Reah, Keith Sanger and
Maggie Bowring

Satellite titles:

Language and Gender
Angela Goddard and Lindsey Meân Patterson

The Language of Advertising: Written texts
(second edition; 2002)
Angela Goddard

The Language of Conversation
Francesca Pridham

The Language of Drama
Keith Sanger

The Language of Fiction
Keith Sanger

The Language of Humour
Alison Ross

The Language of ICT: Information and Communication Technology
Tim Shortis

The Language of Magazines
Linda McLoughlin

The Language of Newspapers
(second edition; 2002)
Danuta Reah

The Language of Poetry
John McRae

The Language of Politics
Adrian Beard

The Language of Speech and Writing
Sandra Cornbleet and Ronald Carter

The Language of Sport
Adrian Beard

Related titles:

Language, Society and Power: An introduction
Linda Thomas, Shân Wareing, Joanna Thornborrow, Jean Stilwell Peccei, Ishtla Singh and Jason Jones

The Television Handbook
(second edition; 2000)
Patricia Holland

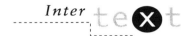

The Language
of Television

◎   Jill Marshall

◎   Angela Werndly

London and New York

First published 2002
by Routledge
11 New Fetter Lane, London EC4P 4EE

Simultaneously published in the USA and Canada
by Routledge
29 West 35th Street, New York, NY 10001

Routledge is an imprint of the Taylor & Francis Group

© 2002 Jill Marshall and Angela Werndly

Typeset in Stone Sans/Stone Serif by
Florence Production Ltd, Stoodleigh, Devon
Printed and bound in Great Britain by
TJ International, Padstow, Cornwall

British Library Cataloguing in Publication Data
A catalogue record for this book is available from the British Library

Library of Congress Cataloging in Publication Data
Marshall, Jill, 1964–
    The language of television / Jill Marshall and Angela Werndly.
        p. cm.—(Intertext)
    Includes bibliographical references and index of terms.
        1. Television broadcasting—Great Britain. 2. Television
    broadcasting—Social aspects—Great Britain. 3. Discourse
    analysis. I. Werndly, Angela, 1954– . II. Title. III. Intertext
    (London, England)
    PN1992.3.G7 M37 2002
    791.45′0941—dc21   2001048820

ISBN 0–415–28794–4 (hbk)
ISBN 0–415–25119–2 (pbk)

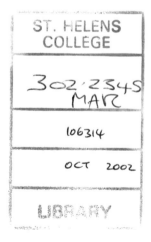

Inter te**X**t

The Language of Television

'Well-constructed and clearly written, this straightforward and accessible introduction will be usable by A-level and first-year undergraduate students alike. The book gives students clear signposts towards ways of thinking about TV as a language, with its own form and content, as well as about some of the discourses and forms of language that we encounter routinely on television.'

Joanna Thornborrow, *Cardiff University, UK*

'This is a comprehensive and rigorous text that remains eminently readable and fascinating. It will be a welcome addition to any English department library.'

Lindsay Foster, *Ryton Comprehensive School, Tyne and Wear, UK*

The INTERTEXT series has been specifically designed to meet the needs of contemporary English Language Studies. *Working with Texts: A core introduction to language analysis* (second edition 2001) is the foundation text, which is complemented by a range of 'satellite' titles. These provide students with hands-on practical experience of textual analysis through special topics and can be used individually or in conjunction with *Working with Texts*.

Aimed at A-Level and beginning undergraduate students, *The Language of Television*:

- ◎ explores a range of genres, from breakfast news to soap operas and 'reality TV';
- ◎ analyses television scheduling and listings;
- ◎ includes extracts from scripts of popular television programmes: *Queer as Folk* and *The Royle Family*;
- ◎ includes a substantial glossary.

Jill Marshall is Lecturer in Communications at Queen Margaret University College, Edinburgh. **Angela Werndly** is Senior Lecturer in Media and Cultural Studies at the University of Sunderland.

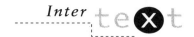

The Intertext series

◎ Why does the phrase 'spinning a yarn' refer both to using language and making cloth?

◎ What might a piece of literary writing have in common with an advert or a note from the milkman?

◎ Which aspects of language are important to understand when analysing texts?

The Routledge INTERTEXT series aims to develop readers' understanding of how texts work. It does this by showing some of the designs and patterns in the language from which they are made, by placing texts within the contexts in which they occur, and by exploring relationships between them.

The series consists of a foundation text, *Working with Texts: A core introduction to language analysis*, which looks at language aspects essential for the analysis of texts, and a range of satellite texts. These apply aspects of language to a particular topic area in more detail. They complement the core text and can also be used alone, providing the user has the foundation skills furnished by the core text.

Benefits of using this series:

◎ **Multi-disciplinary** – provides a foundation for the analysis of texts, supporting students who want to achieve a detailed focus on language.

◎ **Accessible** – no previous knowledge of language analysis is assumed, just an interest in language use.

◎ **Student-friendly** – contains activities relating to texts studied, commentaries after activities, highlighted key terms, suggestions for further reading and an index of terms.

◎ **Interactive** – offers a range of task-based activities for both class use and individual study.

◎ **Tried and tested** – written by a team of respected teachers and practitioners whose ideas and activities have been trialled independently.

contents

acknowledgements

The authors and publishers wish to thank the following for permission to reprint copyright material:

TV listings © Guardian Newspapers Ltd

Dingle Family/Emmerdale photo © Yorkshire Television Ltd

David Beckham photo: courtesy of Actionplus Sports Images

Ali G illustration: courtesy of Alwyn Talbot

Johnson & Johnson advertisement: courtesy of Johnson & Johnson

Best-sellers listing: courtesy of Whitaker BookTrack

Newspaper article: courtesy of *Shields Gazette*

Queer as Folk: The Scripts, Russell T. Davies, 1999: courtesy of C4/Macmillan

The Royle Family, The Scripts: Series I, Caroline Aherne, Craig Cash and Henry Normal, 1999: courtesy of Granada Media

The publishers have made every effort to contact copyright holders although this has not been possible in some cases. Outstanding permissions will be remedied in future editions.

one

What is television?

This unit introduces the medium of television in its historical context and suggests ways in which we can begin to think of the whole medium as having a kind of 'grammar', a rule-governed set of conventions according to which it operates and by which we read or interpret it. One way in which television is offered and read is according to its schedules or programming, as both a vertical menu of programmes throughout the day and as a horizontal selection of programmes across channels, relating to the patterns of our daily lives. A further notion of the way in which television 'speaks' to us as a mediator of the wider world, as a kind of storyteller, is also discussed.

THE HISTORY OF BRITISH TELEVISION

Television broadcasting in Britain began in 1936 but it was suspended during the Second World War and not re-introduced until 1946. For nearly a decade television had only one station, the BBC (the British Broadcasting Corporation), but in 1954 Parliament created the commercially-funded Independent Television Authority, which ended the BBC's monopoly of British television.

1

From the beginning, television output was governed by a philosophy that it should provide a 'public service'. This philosophy was primarily the vision of the first Director General of the BBC, John Reith, who believed that television should provide a service of information, education and entertainment, without direct intervention from government and commerce. Reith's central principle was that the broadcasting of classical music, plays and discussion would educate the viewing public. Although the audience was regarded as active rather than passive, the BBC believed it could and should develop the viewers' listening skills. However, the BBC's belief in, and dedication to, an undivided public good that could be realised through the transmission of predominantly middle-class tastes and values, has been criticised by many scholars in media studies as elitist and patronising.

In terms of television output it meant that the daily menu of each channel consisted of a diverse range of programmes and that repetitious programming was avoided. Popular programmes were mixed with unpopular programmes and, in the early days, transmission breaks were deliberately left between programmes, for example in the early evenings when it was assumed parents should be putting children to bed or helping them with homework.

The aims of 'public service' broadcasting were also reflected in the 1954 Television Act, which ensured that the new commercial station, ITV, offered the same range of programmes as its competitor. When, in 1964, the BBC2 network was launched and, almost two decades later, Channel 4 was introduced to the nation, they had to adhere to the same principles.

In 1986, an investigative panel called the Peacock Committee was set up to produce a report on the BBC licence fee. The report had a massive impact on broadcasting because it recommended deregulation and referred to the audience as consumers who were capable of deciding for themselves what they should watch. As a result satellite broadcasting was introduced to the nation in 1989 by means of the new technologies of a satellite dish and a decoder.

Activity

The programming of British television has been influenced by John Reith's belief that broadcasting should be a service of information, education and entertainment for everyone.

◉   Examine a BBC1 daily television schedule and compare it with a Sky One schedule.

◎ How do the schedules differ?

◎ Can you identify the public service objective to 'inform, educate and entertain' the public in either of the two stations?

(Note: there is no commentary on this activity.)

ASPECTS OF PRODUCTION, TEXTS AND AUDIENCES

As a modern medium, television operates in a production–text–audience cycle. John Thompson, in his book *The Media and Modernity* highlights two important features of media **production**. First, television is a technical medium and so we cannot interact with it or interject in the same way that we do in two-way flow communication such as face-to-face conversation. Secondly, it is **monological** or mass communication, which means that it is not directed at specific individuals but is produced for an unlimited number of people. Like other media, television is capable of multiple reproduction – one television programme can be seen by an unlimited number of people simultaneously.

However, any discussion of the production aspects of television must take the **ownership** of the medium into account. This aspect centres on the relationship between those who own or control television and the television programmes themselves. The British media are not directly in the control of government and theoretically we have politically 'free' media. Nevertheless, recent trends in ownership of the media indicate concentration of ownership. Rupert Murdoch, for example, owns the prominent British broadsheet, *The Times*, and the huge circulation tabloid, the *Sun*, as well as owning BSkyB satellite television and controlling many other media interests in the US and around the world. This has increased concerns amongst people who believe that those who own the media have control over their content. The fact is that only relatively few companies own all media output, which means that, in the course of a single day, we could read newspapers or books and watch television or films that may all be produced by the same multinational company.

The part of television we actually watch and consume is the **text**. The term 'text' is used in media studies to refer to the material that television produces, such as dramas, news, advertisements, documentaries and so on. There are many different approaches to textual analysis, all of which provide insights into the meanings that television texts offer and the **culture** that has produced them. The units in this book explore some of the theories and approaches that are useful for the analysis of texts on television.

Consumption of texts occurs when we switch the television on and we become, at that point, a member of the **audience**. However, the notion of the audience is a complex one. Media research into audiences began in the 1950s in the US with what is now referred to as the **effects model**. This model assumed that the media, including television, were very powerful and that they had a very simple, direct effect upon people's lives. In short, it was believed that meanings in media texts were received by an audience in a very passive way. In the 1960s this notion of media effects was reversed and a new model, the **uses and gratifications** approach was developed. This model assumed that the individuals in the audience determined their own selection and use of media texts and meanings which they used to gratify certain needs, such as finding a diversion from everyday life, and that the media had little power.

A more recent way of studying audiences, rejecting both these models, was developed in British media and cultural studies. It provides a method whereby researchers observe and then analyse the ways in which specific audiences relate to the medium of television, taking into account both the capacity of audiences to negotiate meanings and uses of television, and the power of television as a medium and as an industry. Specific examples of this kind of research and the insights it yields regarding television viewers are discussed in Units three and five.

The perception of 'audience' now is that we are not an undifferentiated 'mass' who passively receive television messages. Rather, the audience is seen as comprising various social groups in terms of age, social class, gender, sexuality and ethnicity, who are all active in reading and interpreting television texts.

THE TEXTUAL LANDSCAPE OF TELEVISION

The meanings of television for us are, in part, related to **scheduling** which regulates what and when we watch. The British terrestrial channels are organised according to **vertical** and **horizontal** patterns of television programming. Television broadcasting is organised around individual, relatively self-contained units – programmes – and these are, to an extent, organised vertically. In 1958, theorist Raymond Williams proposed that an evening's viewing was presented as a kind of menu. We can still see this menu on terrestrial television. We could, for instance, examine five days' programming on the BBC and see these vertical patterns: soap opera, news and drama occupy particular spaces in what Williams called the vertical 'flow', while situation comedies are common in prime time and low-budget cult comic shorts pepper the post-midnight spaces.

Awareness of vertical continuity is demonstrated when, at teatime, we are shown carefully selected clips from late-night programmes that are deemed suitable for any viewer regardless of age. Such awareness also often appears in the texts, as when the host of a satirical panel game assures us that the censored swearing will be restored in the late-night repeat. This means that, not only do we organise our own evening's viewing vertically, but we also scan across the channels at, for example, 6.30 p.m. and select from soaps and dramas aimed at the younger viewer. Indeed, we can do this in other time bands, because programming is similar across the channels throughout twenty-four hours.

There are signs though that this is changing, as television organises itself more horizontally across digital, cable and online channels. Specialised cable channels such as Paramount Comedy, MTV, Trouble, Travel, and Food and Drink, operate outside this vertical flow. It is important to remember that television texts are never isolated from the texts around them and, therefore, the concept of flow remains useful when considering both texts and audiences. You may have experience of digital on-screen menus for cable channels which organise your programme guides across all the many channels, both horizontally and vertically, as well as by programme type. We can think of scheduling and viewing patterns as part of the grammar of television.

Activity

Read Text: TV guide overleaf and identify how the schedules are presented or may be used:

◎   vertically

◎   horizontally

Text: TV guide

Television | Wednesday 6

Wednesday 6 | Television

watch this ⬤⬤

BBC1

6.0 Breakfast (T) 71752 9.0 Kilroy (T) (S) News (T) 76490 10.0 City Hospital (T) (S) 764032 **11.0** Garden Invaders (T) (S) 3099 **11.30** House Invaders (T) (S) News (T) 4728 **12.0** Playing For Time (T) (S) 36591 **12.30** Going For A Song (T) (S) 62273 **1.0** News (T) Weather 88612 **1.45** Neighbours (T) (S) 3486603 **2.05** Bergerac (T) (S) 5449342 **2.55** Through The Keyhole (T) (S) **3.25** CBBC: Tweenies **3.45** Dennis The Menace (T) (S) 5238 **4.10** The Wild Thornberrys (T) (S) 3896525 **5.0** Blue Peter (T) (S) 6294099 **5.25** Newsround (T) (S) 4966070 **5.35** Neighbours (T) (S) (R) 369825

6.0 BBC News (T) 341
6.30 Regional News Weather 693
7.0 Animal Hospital (T) (S) A kitten that was put in a microwave. 6728
7.30 Match Of The Day Live (T) Greece v England (Kick-off 7.45pm) World Cup qualifying match in Athens. 20064964

9.55 The Midweek National Lottery Draw With Lottery Extra (T) (S) Presented by Brenda Emmanus. 328898

10.0 BBC News At Ten O'Clock (T) Weather 80772 National Lottery Update. 709167
10.40 80 Years A Queen Celebration (T) Shirley Bassey, Lionel Ritchie and Hear'Say sing some songs to celebrate Prince Philip's 80th birthday. Weatherview 9114594
12.0 Tomorrow's World Mountain Madness (T) (R) 4126 **12.30** Panorama (T) (R) 3948804 **1.20** A History of Britain (T) (R) 7975842 **2.20** See Hear! (S) (R) 8770007 **3.05** BBC News 24 24475255

BBC2

6.0 Wiggly Park (T) (R) 7749052 **7.05** Playdays (T) (S) (R) 4976709 **7.25** Pocket Dragon (T) (S) 7352766 **7.35** Smurfs (T) (S) 226673 **8.0** So/So (T) (R) 7322780 **8.25** The Puppy (T) (R) 6886254 **8.45** Oakie Doke (T) (S) 5967078 Vote 2001: Election Call (T) 1289031 **9.45** Watch (T) 4329760 **10.0** Teletubbies (T) (S) (R) 4935 **10.30** Tweenies (T) (S) 4996709 **10.50** Watch (T) (S) **11.0** English Express (T) 1124109 **11.30** Look And Read (T) 3325490 Landmarks (T) 1559501 **12.30** Working Lunch (T) 6082 **1.0** Oakie Doke (T) (R) 3984254 **1.10** The Turtles Of Tahiti (Charles Vidor, 1942) (T) Comedy starring Charles Laughton, Jon Hall. 3215513 **2.40** Vote 2001: Campaign Live (T) 8256273 **3.30** Esther (T) (S) 7659 **4.30** Ready Steady Cook (T) (S) (R) 1394815

6.0 TOTP 2 Roxy Music Special (T) (S) 379362
6.45 Star Trek: Deep Space Nine Field of Fire (T) (S) 256054
7.30 The Englishman Who Went Up A Hill, But Came Down A Mountain (Chris Monger, 1995) (T) Drama starring Hugh Grant. See Film Choice. 57732

9.0 Inside Clouds: A Drink And Drugs Clinic The Staff (T) Two members of staff at the prestigious rehabilitation clinic in Wiltshire give therapy to the residents. Their advice is all the more valuable as it comes from past experience of their own addiction nightmares but, despite the help, some just don't want to hear. 8419

10.0 Residents (T) (S) Tina begins her new life. 34902
10.30 Newsnight (T) (S) 350032
11.20 World Amateur Boxing Championships 86896
12.0 Northern Lights: The Devil You Know (T) 8437961 **12.10** Tartan Shorts (T) (S) (R) 64920 **12.0** BBC Learning Zone Out: Flexible Work — Insecure Lives 26461 **1.0** Ever Relationships 89756681 **1.50** Ever Wondered? 728097 **2.40** Languages: Talk Spanish 7=6 6969 **5.0** Working In Sport And Leisure: Thinking And Number Skills 2013 **6.0** OU: Shooting Video History 744910

ITV

6.0 GMTV 7879428 9.25 Trisha (T) (S) 2493549 **10.30** This Morning (T) 1555283 **12.0** ITV Lunchtime News Including Local News And ITV Weather (T) 67373 **12.30** Survival Guide (T) (S) 98983 **1.0** London Today (T) Weather 7780 **1.29** City Survival Guide 6798582 **1.30** Crossroads (T) (S) 6662 **2.0** Live Talk (T) 9380 **2.28** City Survival Guide 2459342 **2.30** Blue Heelers (T) 780 **3.0** ITV News Headlines (T) City Survival Guide 8578623 **3.05** London Today; (T) Weather 1296453 **3.16** City Survival Guide 8568293 **3.20** CITV: Dream Street (T) 8356419 **3.30** Mopatop's Shop (T) (S) (R) 1876612 **3.40** Hound Spanking New Doug (T) 2096624 **4.05** Scooby And Scrappy Doo (T) (R) 764287 **4.15** Brilliant Creatures The Teenage Witch (T) (S) 7966490 **5.05** Crossroads (T) (S) (R) 7708083 **5.35** Wheel Of Fortune (T) (S) 289983

6.0 London Tonight (T) Weather 709
6.30 ITV Evening News (T) Weather 761
7.0 Emmerdale (T) (S) Paddy catches Zoe and Charity in a compromising situation. 1896
7.30 Coronation Street (T) Alma throws a farewell dinner party. 273

8.0 Poirot The ABC Murders (T) (S) (R) The dapper Belgian sleuth receives several anonymous letters outlining a killer's intention to murder a string of people in alphabetical order, beginning with Alice Ascher of Andover. Let's hope he's got a phone book 9525

10.0 ITV News At Ten Including Local News And ITV Weather (T) 38728
10.30 Real Crime: The Hunt For Wearside Jack The hunt for the man behind one of the biggest hoaxes in British history. 8135983
11.35 Mean Streets (Martin Scorsese, 1973) (T) Gritty New York drama starring Robert De Niro, Harvey Keitel, Amy Robinson. See Film Choice. 2889773
1.40 Cyber... (T) (R) 5444184 **2.10** Trisha (T) (S) 99503 **3.30** Thriller starring Patrick Holt. Honor Blackman, Emrys Jones. 684216 **4.10** ITV Nightscreen (T) 87582845 **5.30** News 40587

Channel 4

6.0 Ivor The Engine (T) (R) 3591506 **6.05** The Hoobs (T) (R) 498449 **6.30** The Hoobs (T) (R) 4305 **7.0** The Big Breakfast 7825 **8.0** 4Learning: Rat-a-Tat-Tat 4236692 **8.45** Bewitched (T) (R) 15679 **9.30** Rat-a-Tat-Tat 982380 **9.50** The Number Crew 4042083 **10.0** Stage One 498900 **10.15** All About Us 779094 **10.30** The English Programme 488687 **10.50** The Number Crew II

11.25 First Edition 715587 **11.40** Conquering The Normans 4474149 **12.0** Powerhouse (T) 559 **12.30** Watercolour Challenge (T) 55987 **1.0** D-Day, The Sixth Of June (Henry Koster, 1956) (T) Drama starring Robert Taylor. 558963 **3.30** Revealing Secrets (T) (R) 74573 **4.30** Great Estates (T) (R) 79632 **5.0** Pet Rescue (T) 9024 **5.25** Big Brother (T) (R) 16q6099

6.0 Friends The One Where Ross Finds Out (T) (R) Rachel gets drunk. 821
6.30 Hollyoaks (T) R) How forensic evidence helped solve the case of a fatal pipe bomb attack on a judge. 6284285
7.0 News (T) Including sport and weather. 9971

8.0 Brookside (T) Nisha tells Jerome they're finished. 8186
8.30 Nigella Bites (T) Nigella Lawson makes an Elvis-style fried peanut butter and banana sandwich. 7693
9.0 ER Witch Hunt (T) An infant under Abby's care disappears from the hospital. Meanwhile, Greene learns the results of his competency test, and a suicidal woman accuses Legaspi of sexual harassment. 6815

10.0 Big Brother (T) 79070
10.30 The Twisted Lives Of Contortionists (T) The flexible world of athletes able to bend and twist their bodies into extraordinary shapes. 9322
11.30 Chance (T) (S) Mike takes a spin at the stock market. 6585 **12.0** Spin City (T) (R) 779702 **12.30** 5 (T) (R) 5751 **1.30** Politics Isn't Working: The Dumbed-Down Election (T) (R) 3347676 **2.25** Politics Isn't Working (T) 6260642 **3.40** Trans World Sport (T) (R) 226643 **4.35** Countdown (T) (R) 698575 **5.05** Powerhouse (T) 4964754 **5.30** Countdown (T) (S) (R) 4829

Channel 5

6.0 News (S) 7776457 **7.0** Milkshake! (S) 84826517 **7.05** Mr Men And Little Miss (S) (R) 8947327 **7.10** The Big Breakfast 782838 **7.20** Animal Antics (S) (R) 772066 **8.0** Havakazoo (S) (R) 9358 **8.25** Toluca Polla Ole (S) (R) 835506 **7.55** Bear In The Big Blue House (S) (R) 8235448 **8.25** Beachcomber Bay (S) (R) 826635 **8.50** Ricki Lake (T) (S) 226425 **9.35** The Wright Stuff (S) 2978902 **10.30** The Bold And The Beautiful (T) (S) 9757308 **10.55** Charlie's Angels (T) (S) (R) 4803782 **12.0** 5 News At Noon; (T) (S) Weather 1960051 **12.30** Family Affairs (T) (S) 827051 **1.0** The Oprah Winfrey Show (S) (R) 16211070 **1.60** 100 Per Cent (S) 4490498 **2.20** Open House With Gloria Hunniford (T) (S) 829621 **3.35** The World's Most Daring Rescues (S) (R) 4679592 **4.15** Family Affairs (T) (S) 7756634 **4.45** Live International Football (T) (S) Estonia v Republic Of Ireland. 91979693

7.05 News Sport 5 (T) (S) Weather 354525
7.30 Murder Detectives Deadly Delivery (R) How forensic evidence helped solve the case of a disturbing gift. 621

8.0 Jumpin' Jack Flash (Penny Marshall, 1986) (T) Implausible but fun comedy about a computer programmer who somehow gets drawn into a spy caper. Starring Whoopi Goldberg, Jonathan Pryce, Carol Kane, Jim Belushi, Roscoe Lee Browne. 28406q3

10.0 Rambo: First Blood Part II (George P an Cosmatos, 1985) (T) (S) Superadimb action with Sylvester Stallone single-handedly re-fighting the Vietnam War. With Richard Crenna, Charles Napier, Steven Berkoff. See Film Choice. 3758490
11.55 The Comedy Store (S) New and established stand-up performers, featuring Tim Vine, Dave Johns, Andrew Pipe and Patrice O'Neal. 608658
12.25 The'70s Show Kitty and Eric's emotional blackmail and jealousy. 3333200 **12.55** Live Major League Baseball (S) 4395326 **4.30** Aussie Rules Football (S) 4096600 **5.30** 100 Per Cent (S) (R) 445709

TOTP2
6pm, C4
For the first time since 1983, Roxy Music are doing The Strand (and others) in front of a live audience for this TOTP2 special, a warm-up for their world tour revival which starts next week. FV

Nigella Bites
8.30pm, C4
Nigella's food odyssey continues, this week providing a culinary parallel between food and fashion, as we alight in the land of trash. So it's on with the stonewash jeans and Elvis glasses for a feast of what turns out to be basically high-fat comfort food, mostly originating from America's deep south. Included are the king's authentic-looking fried peanut butter and banana sandwiches, ham cooked in cola, deep fried chicken and more, and all seem straightforward to make. But once again Nigella world, peopled with beaming children and witty, daiquiri-drinking chums, makes you feel thoroughly inadequate, and distracts from the overall message — enjoy your food BC

Residents
10pm, BBC2
In the final episode of this darkest of comedies, things aren't going well for some of the suburban inhabitants. Then again, when did they ever go well? While Sally cheats on Dave, Ranjit faces ruin because of problems with the insurance company, and Roger is being stalked by a newly sober and apparently murderous Hilary. Against this chaotic background, Guy gives in to Tony's emotional blackmail and Eric's Banjo to organise a stag night that, inevitably and inexorably, ends badly. Savage to the point of being downright nasty. Roll on season two. JW

Film choice
● **The Englishman Who Went Up A Hill But Came Down A Mountain**
7.30pm, BBC2
● **Rambo: First Blood II** 10pm, C5
● **Mean Streets** 11.35pm, ITV
The week's best films, page 54

(R) Repeat (S) Stereo (T) Teletext

Jun 2-8 2001

In these television pages, the vertical and horizontal menus of programming are apparent because each of the five terrestrial channels is listed according to time bands. We can see what is on each channel for the whole day but we can also look across the channels at, for example, 9 p.m. 'prime time' and see that we are offered major documentaries, 'concept' programmes (those based around a single strong idea or situation such as the UK's *Big Brother*) and high-production sitcoms and dramas. We can see that in other time bands, programming is similar across the channels; for instance 'magazine' shows – programmes with lots of separate segments – are offered at breakfast-time and later in the morning. These programmes are designed to be comprehensible if you are watching only portions of them (rather than watching all the way through) because people will be doing things like getting ready for work or looking after children, while they are broadcast.

Soap operas are typically offered in the after-school/work slots at 5–6.30 p.m. and in the early evening after-dinner slots. The more broadly popular a programme is designed to be, such as a family sitcom, the more likely it is that it will be scheduled during the 8–10 p.m. prime time. Programmes likely to appeal to small, specialised audiences are often scheduled very late at night. One thing this guide couldn't show was that television is not quite fixed in terms of scheduling: because sentence was passed that day on the notorious Shipman murder case, the programming that night was disrupted or ran late due to the broadcast of extended news programmes and documentaries.

Look at today's television guide and watch some of today's programmes. Identify any examples of the segmentation of programming you encounter.

Relate notions of vertical and horizontal programming and segmentation to people's daily routines and think about how this informs and affects the programme choices they make.

7

TELEVISION AS A DOMESTIC MEDIUM

A lot of our time at home is taken up with watching television and research has shown that, in general, we spend more time viewing television programmes than on any other leisure pursuit, including going to the cinema, listening to CDs or even playing computer games. In Britain, ninety-eight per cent of homes own at least one television and there are 19.3 million television licences.

Television use has changed over the years. Longer television days and developments in technology, such as the video recorder, the remote control and satellite television, have brought about different patterns in the use of television in British homes. We now have more control over what we watch and when we watch it; we are more likely to have access to more than one television set per household; we can surf the stations or switch channels during commercial breaks; and we can even use the television to play computer games or send e-mails.

The context of television viewing has also changed in recent years. At one time we could say that it differed from other forms of the media, such as the cinema, because it was never used in the public domain. However, today, television is part of the public environment of pubs and clubs where a big screen allows us to watch a soap wedding or the FA Cup Final outside the boundaries of the domestic context.

We use the television for a variety of reasons, many of which will be discussed in forthcoming chapters, but it is important to stress here that it is not a time-wasting activity. For example, we rely on television, especially television news, as a source of information about what is going on in the wider social world. Television also has an important function as entertainment; television viewing figures, which are published in the national press weekly, consistently demonstrate the popularity of fictional programmes such as soaps, dramas and sitcoms.

Activity

Over the course of a week, keep a record of the amount of time you and other members of your household spend watching television. Also keep a record of whether you watch a programme alone (for example, in your bedroom) or with other household members. You may find that you and the people you live with watch television more than you thought.

(Note: there is no commentary on this activity.)

TELEVISION AS 'STORYTELLER'

Although it is a mass communication medium, television can be related to much older forms of verbal communication. In 1978, media theorists Fiske and Hartley argued that television has a social communication role similar to that of the bards or storytellers of older tribal societies. In these communities, the storyteller or bard was a medium through which the wider culture would have been relayed to people. The role of the story-teller was, therefore, not so much as an inventor of new stories but as someone who interpreted and passed on narratives – stories – explaining the wider world to an audience. The storytelling role belongs to an oral – spoken – tradition of language use in culture rather than a written tradition, so the storyteller is a 'voice' which mediates the wider culture for the community.

The storyteller, in this model, is someone who is at the centre of a community and who serves as a focus for making sense of events and ideas according to certain sets of values which are dominant in that community. Fiske and Hartley argued that television can be thought of as fulfilling a similar mediating role. It acts to interpret the wider world, to bind society together in a consensus about what is real and what is important, and to reproduce some kind of social consensus about events and ideas.

For instance, the evening television news acts as a way of informing us about all the 'events' of the day, but typically lasts only half an hour. The news, therefore, selects only events that are recent, shocking or important enough to appear as news items. It also presents news in such a way that events are spoken about within a very broad social consensus: if we are told that the Prime Minister has been campaigning for a general election and has had an egg thrown at him, the newsreader will not volunteer an opinion that he deserved it. This is because such an opinion reveals a party political allegiance which only some of the audience will share. Instead, the incident will be reported 'neutrally', i.e. the news-reader will not voice any opinion. It may be that a prime minister somewhere else in the world has also been pelted with an egg on the same day, but it will probably not make the news in Britain.

Another example of social consensus can be seen in the ways in which British soap operas have changed over the years, remembering that the oldest UK soap – *Coronation Street* – has been broadcast for more than forty years. Soaps did not, until the 1980s, feature black or gay characters as part of their central 'communities', but now they do. Thus they reproduce social changes in Britain whereby ethnic minority populations have grown and become more important to the culture, and where gay relationships are looked upon more positively than they once were. (Having gay relationships was illegal in Britain until 1967.) Assuming a broad social consensus in a culture is not the same as saying that everyone in that culture has the same views; clearly they don't. At any one time, however, some viewpoints are dominant in society.

Soap opera is an example of how cultural events and ideas are made sense of in the languages of television. These 'languages' generally consist of both verbal language and images. This is in some ways similar to the way that bards once made sense of a wider culture and history through songs and stories. Soap communities, whether they are streets, villages, squares or hotels, are meant to represent, to some extent, lots of communities in our culture. However, the narratives lived out by soap characters, whilst representing 'ordinary' everyday life, do not mirror our experiences of actual everyday life in timescale or events, but select and condense only some events into stories. We would not watch a drama of people sleeping for eight hours, which is what happens in actual everyday life. Even in 'reality TV' programming, a well-known example of which is *Big Brother*, we don't all want to watch unedited 'reality'.

In this storytelling or 'bardic' model, Fiske and Hartley also emphasise the extent to which television allows us to make sense of our culture as well as 'foreign' or 'outside' cultures. As a twenty-first-century nation, we live very differently from historic tribal communities, so television may act for us as a point of focus and contact between groups of people who otherwise live unconnected lives. We can imagine, however, that if the medium does not seem to include or represent us or our views – if we come from a different ethnic background than television programmes assume, or because we are much younger or older than the age group the medium seems to be speaking to – we will not necessarily feel culturally involved.

In our society, people have different and unequal relationships with a mass medium like television. Some people hold privileged positions in relation to it, such as television producers, or television critics and academics who may believe that they have a right to try and influence programming. Most of us may feel ourselves less able to influence television output, although we still enjoy or object to it in a variety of ways.

Activity

What does the language in Text: Review taken from a national broadsheet newspaper tell us about the kinds of assumptions the review makes about soap operas? What seems to be the reason for publishing this kind of commentary about a television programme?

SOAPS CAN BE BRILLIANT and they can be brilliantly bad but they should never be just boring. . . . the summer – when half the audience is away on holiday – is a period of nothing, of consolidation, waiting for the big storylines to go off in the build-up to Christmas. So, Greg Kelly and Steve Owen are safely behind bars. Illicit loves between Susannah Farnham and Greg Shadwick, Mike Baldwin and Linda, Maxine and Ashley, and Bianca and Desperate Dan, have all begun to grow stale. The resolution of Nikki Shadwick's rape has been postponed due to lack of interest and Lindsay Corkhill's minder has kept her under control. *EastEnders* has been padding its storylines out with Terry's karaoke career, Pat's version of *Changing Rooms* and entertaining ways of Irene saying 'Fong-Shoo-Way'.

Commentary

The language of the review tells us two things in particular. The critic is positioning him-/herself as a commentator on soap in the same way that viewers typically do, critiquing storylines and commenting on characters: 'Illicit loves between Susannah Farnham and Greg Shadwick, Mike Baldwin and Linda (. . .) have all begun to grow stale.' The critic also uses plenty of names and detail about the soaps which indicates an 'insider knowledge' of them, a gossipy characteristic which is part of the viewing ritual of soaps. However, the commentary is open to an ironic interpretation – 'The resolution of Nikki Shadwick's rape has been postponed due to lack of interest (. . .)' – which indicates a way of viewing soaps from a position of enjoyable superiority:

'Soaps can be brilliant and . . . brilliantly bad (. . .)'. The critic not only dispar-
ages the characters, but steps back further to critique aspects of the process
of soap production by putting the remarks in the context of comments that
the TV industry has a reason for letting the texts become boring: the summer
audience is away, so the production companies will put their efforts into
pulling in audiences for the autumn ratings battles.

Activity

Compare and contrast the language in Text: Letter, published in a fortnightly
magazine dedicated to soap operas and their viewers, with Text: Review
(above). What differences do you observe? What seems to be the reason for
publishing this kind of commentary about a television programme?

(Note: there is no commentary on this activity.)

Text: Letter

What wouldn't I give to be Irene Raymond in *EastEnders*.
At the first sign of a hot flush and mid-life crisis, she books herself
into a health farm. I'm sure a lot of other ladies like myself who
have reached a certain age would just love to be able to treat
themselves to an expensive luxury like that. Then again, I suppose
when you live with Terry you deserve a break!

Activity

Fiske and Hartley's 'bardic' model (see p. 9) was proposed at a time when
home VCR ownership was in its early days, before the mass take-up of cable,
satellite and digital television broadcasting, and before DVD and home Internet
access. Discuss whether you think the 'bardic' model is still relevant now.

(Note: there is no commentary on this activity.)

SUMMARY

This unit has introduced students to the history of television and the concept of public service broadcasting. It has discussed television from the aspects of production, text and audience, and has also presented a way of reading or analysing television in terms of the vertical, horizontal and segmented patterns of programming.

Television as a domestic medium has been explored and the unit has also explained and invited critical analysis of the idea that television fulfils a socially binding mediating role somewhat similar to the oral tradition of the community storyteller.

Finally, the unit indicated the growing 'extensions' of the television landscape into the new media such as digital television and the Internet.

Extension

Look on the Internet for television-related web sites. What is their typical content? What do you think is their main purpose? In particular, what do you judge to be the main differences between 'official' broadcasters' web sites and 'unofficial' fan sites?

13

Signs and signification

This unit will demonstrate the principles of **semiotics**, as they apply to language as a sign system, and to visual sign systems. This is in order to contextualise meaning in television texts.

SIGNIFICATION

One way of studying meaning in language is to look at what words might mean, but we can also examine *how* spoken or written words are able to communicate meaning to the listener or reader. This kind of analysis is called semiotics, which means 'the study of signs'. A semiotic analysis can also be used to investigate how other types of communication, such as film and television images, work in a similar way to language.

In semiotics, elements of language, such as words, are referred to as **signs**, and they work together as part of a **sign system**. For example English words work together within the general sign system of the English language. A language proper, like English, is a very complex sign system, but other, simpler sign systems work in a similar way, governed by similar basic rules and conventions. The way we use colours to mean things is an example of the way a simple sign system works. For instance, in a variety of situations, colours have specific significance based on the

15

various meanings our culture associates with them, and we use them like a simple language.

Blood is red, for example, and so red in Western cultures is seen to be an aggressive colour and is used both as a warning, such as in the sign system used for road traffic, and to **signify** passion, as in the gift of a red rose. In traffic signs, green, the colour of nature and harmony, is used opposite red to mean 'safe to go'. Perhaps because we associate darkness and 'the night' with death, clothes and other trappings at funerals are black to acknowledge mourning, whereas at carnivals we put together as many bright, primary colours as possible. Colours are often given meanings arbitrarily because of old customs like dressing babies in 'blue for a boy, pink for a girl', and we still think of pink as a 'girls' colour' (or, now, as a girl-power colour).

So colours can be put together in such simple language-like systems in which they are **symbolic**, that is they represent or 'stand in for' other, more complicated things and ideas. Lots of things are used in this way as sign systems which have cultural meanings. Our choice of clothes, for example, the kinds of cars we drive, or the kinds of ways in which we decorate our houses and gardens. We often feel we can tell something about a person because of her or his choices of these things.

Activity

We use clothes and other personal possessions as a sign system, a kind of language to say things about ourselves. They say something about, for example, our personality, our social status, our role at work or our membership of cultural groups, e.g. as sports or music fans.

◎   Look at the characters' clothes in Text: *Emmerdale* cast opposite and decide what they mean.

◎   Think of further examples, from your own experience, of the meanings of certain types of clothes, cars or other things we buy.

(Note: there is no commentary on this activity.)

Text: *Emmerdale cast*

SEMIOTIC ANALYSIS

Investigation of the more complex relationships between words and meaning can begin with the same notion that they are symbols, used to represent the world for us. If we take the English word 'rose' as an example of a sign to explore using semiotics, it would be necessary to break it down into two elements of meaning, termed the **signifier** and the **signified**. The signifier is the element which we can see or hear, either the marks on the page which make up the written word 'rose', or the sound of the word being spoken. The signified is the element which we can't see or hear, which is the idea or feeling which the signifier brings to our minds.

In Western cultures a semiotic analysis of 'rose' can be represented like this:

Signifier + Signified   = Sign

Rose   Understanding the
                word makes us think
                of the flower

This communicates understanding to an English speaker from a Western culture. In semiotics, written or spoken words are referred to as arbitrary signifiers because they have no natural relationship with what they are representing; they are just random symbols and sounds which we use to make meaning. However, a signifier does not have to be a written or spoken word. It can be, for example, a picture such as a drawing or photograph of a rose:

Signifier + Signified   = Sign

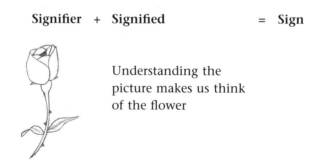

Understanding the
picture makes us think
of the flower

These are iconic signifiers, which means that they do have a relationship with what they represent – they look like the things they are representations of. Let's take the example of a human face:

There are degrees of **iconicity**.

(a)   A 'smiley':

(b)   The 'emotive icons' – 'emoticons' – made up from keyboard strokes
used in e-mails and text messages:

:-)   happy

:-(sad

:-o   shock

:-?   'uh-oh'

These are very simplistic or stylised representations of human faces,
whereas a photographic or video image looks very much more like a real
face.

Activity

◎   Look at the picture in Text: Beckham shown overleaf and identify as
many examples as you can of arbitrary and iconic signifiers.

◎   What do you think the signified is for each of these signifiers?

◎   Can you explain how the signifiers in the photo relate to one another,
inform one another, making the whole photo a piece of communication?

19

Text: Beckham

This photograph shows the footballer David Beckham in action. The photographic image of Beckham is an iconic signifier, the signified of which is our idea of 'David Beckham', or, at a broader level, our idea of 'a footballer'. It has a high degree of iconicity because images reproduced on film (still or moving) or videotape look very much like the things they represent. A humorous cartoon of Beckham in a newspaper would also be an iconic signifier of him, although it would be less iconic than a photograph. A drawing or painting of Beckham made by a child would still be an iconic signifier; it would have a natural relationship with the real thing, even though it might not look very much like him.

The writing 'Beckham' on the footballer's shirt, however, is an arbitrary signifier of him, bearing no natural relationship to the person. The logos around the pitch are also arbitrary signifiers, their signifieds being the companies advertised.

Arbitrary signification – language – works with visual signification here to communicate that the footballer pictured kicking the ball is in fact Beckham and, because this player is a well-known star, that gives the photo particular meaning. If we could see them, the colours of his strip – red and white – would signify his team Manchester United, and the number on Beckham's back shows his squad number. The prominent logos on the players' shirts and around the pitch tell us who is sponsoring the match and tell us that football is not just a game but also a commercial enterprise.

Identify arbitrary and iconic signifiers, such as pictures and words, in the picture overleaf. Decide on the degree of iconicity of each signifier.

What are their signifieds and how do the various signifiers and their signifieds work together to make the whole picture meaningful?

(Note: there is no commentary on this activity.)

Text: Ali G

VISUAL SIGNIFICATION

Signs are rarely seen in isolation. They usually appear with other signs and are organised in particular ways to communicate meaning. The process of formulating a message involves selection and combination. We select from sets of signs, or **paradigms**, and combine them in **syntagms**. An example often used to illustrate this process is when we place an order at a restaurant. To do this we first read the menu and then select from the paradigm of dishes on offer. Let us say that the paradigm for starters is garlic bread, prawn cocktail and potato wedges; the main course paradigm consists of seafood pizza, spaghetti bolognese and

vegetarian risotto; and the dessert paradigm is banana split and choco-
late fudge cake. Our selections from these paradigms, combined to make
up our order for garlic bread, vegetarian risotto and a banana split is a
syntagm which is our complete meal. It has been constructed according
to certain rules and conventions – we wouldn't think of ordering a
banana split, as a main course because it would flout the rules or manners
of dining out.

We can say, then, that signs have a structural relationship.

LOUDLY WALLS MUSIC THE WAS THROUGH BLASTING THE

The reason that this combination makes no sense is because words have
been put in the wrong order, even though they are from the right word
classes. As we have seen with the example of a menu, there are rules and
conventions which govern how signs are put together in order to make
meaning. The grammar of the English language is an example of a set
of such rules. We select words from paradigms and combine them in
syntagms to produce meaning:

MY (NOUN) BOUGHT A SPORTS CAR

We would select an appropriate word from the paradigm of nouns
such as MOTHER, GRANNY, BROTHER or BOYFRIEND to complete this
sentence, which is our syntagm. The meaning of the sentence depends
on our choice of noun because each noun is different from the others.

Television, like film, is a medium of moving images, usually combined with spoken language. Shot either on film or video, television
pictures consist of a moving series of iconic signifiers. A television text
is constructed through a process that involves selecting images from paradigms and combining them into syntagms according to rules and
conventions.

There is a grammar of moving images which functions like
grammar in language. For example, the camera angle used to film a shot
is a signifier.

The close-up is used often in soap opera scenes because it communicates the relationships between people and invites us to concentrate
on the emotions or feelings of a character. On the other hand, the long
shot is used more in texts such as action films where spectacle and visual
effects are emphasised. A shot taken from below the eye level of a character emphasises their power because our perspective is as if we are
looking up at them.

Settings, people and lighting are also important signs. For example, the UK television text *2.4 Children* was a sitcom about a family. The selected signs were of a family consisting of a mother, father and their teenage son and daughter. The text's chosen signs for the family also included settings, such as a semi-detached suburban house, and included situations, such as family mealtimes. These are all signs from a paradigm we could call 'family life' which make up a syntagm which, to an extent, idealises traditional 'family life'.

If we contrast these signs with those chosen from *Absolutely Fabulous*, another UK sitcom about a family, we can see that they are very different. In *Absolutely Fabulous*, the family consists of a single mother with a career, her teenage daughter, a grandmother and a close female friend who is always in the house. The setting is an upmarket residence in a fashionable part of London and situations rarely include traditional family mealtimes. The signs selected here are combined to produce a very different syntagm which makes *Absolutely Fabulous* a far more subversive commentary on 'family life'.

In a visual narrative, shots are combined to produce scenes and scenes are combined to construct a **narrative**. Narrative is the organisation of a story and is a feature of non-fictional as well as fictional texts. The strategies governing the organisation of a narrative depend on certain codes and conventions that enable us to recognise movement through time and space. The most familiar narratives are constructed with a beginning–middle–end structure or, more precisely, with movement from an established situation through a disruption to a new established situation (for an account of this see Unit three). We can observe this narrative structure in many texts, such as romance novels, where we read about a heroine who meets and is immediately attracted to a male character, but who experiences a series of problems and misunderstandings before finally agreeing to marry him.

Popular television programmes also have this structure. For example, quiz shows begin with the host introducing the competitors to the audience, then they move on to the excitement and spectacle of the competition itself during which people compete with each other, usually gaining or losing money, before finally concluding by confirming the winners. Detective dramas usually have this structure, too. They begin with images of normal life and tranquillity which are disrupted by a violent event, such as a murder or robbery. The narrative then progresses through the actions of the detective who finally captures, or deduces the identity of, the criminal to achieve a resolution to the narrative.

Activity

Watch at least one programme currently on television which is a detective drama. Does it follow the narrative structure outlined above? Identify aspects of its usual formula.

(Note: there is no commentary on this activity.)

Activity

Analyse the production of meaning in Text: Storyboard (produced at the planning stage for a film or television sequence) as a series of shots – visual signifiers – which combine to make a narrative sequence.

Text: Storyboard

Commentary

The storyboard is a sequence of images which are the opening moments of a television text, over which a music soundtrack plays. The first image is a man looking down at something. The second is a bird's-eye view of a city landscape. The third is a long shot of the man entering a building, and the next is a medium shot of the man in a room talking to a police officer. The final shot is a close-up of the man with a grim expression.

This succession of images forms a narrative. We assume that the man is looking at the city and that the building is a particular one in that same community. There is nothing on the storyboard to show that the interior shot is from inside the same building, but we are able to **read** this meaning because we understand narrative codes and conventions. Similarly, we recognise that the sequence of images denoting the man and the police officer depicts them in conversation, and that the concerned look on the man's face is a response to some information he has been given. Scenes which show conversations often give us a shot from one character's point of view followed by a shot from the other character's view of the first character and so on. This is known as a shot/reverse shot sequence.

Such visual signifiers are produced during shooting but there are further devices produced during the editing process, such as the dissolving or fragmenting of the picture, which can signify a dream sequence or series of flashbacks to past events. Split-screen narrative devices in which we can see different scenes unfolding simultaneously and slow-motion shots which may signify a key narrative event are all signifiers created by editing.

Activity

Select the opening title sequence of a popular television programme. This could be a police show such as *The Bill* (UK), a medical drama such as *Casualty* or *A&E* (both UK), or a quiz show. Analyse its meanings as a series of visual and other signifiers.

Look at a television news broadcast. Work out how the meaning of the newsreader's words depends on visual signification such as still backdrop images or film footage of an event.

The title sequence you choose will probably combine its visual language with written language, such as the programme title and credits, and sound, such as music. Television texts are dependent for their meaning on a combination of language – mainly spoken – and visual signification. We cannot analyse the language spoken on television without taking account of the signifying context in which it occurs. For instance, if a character in a television drama speaks the line 'I feel uncomfortable here', its meaning for the audience depends on visual signification. If a newsreader says, 'There have been rumblings here throughout the day', as part of a voice-over, its meaning depends on whether the video is of London Zoo or of the House of Commons.

Explain how meaning in the utterances given in the following script, Text: *Queer as Folk*, depends in part on the context of visual signification also given as instructions in the script.

Comment on the extent to which it is apparent that visual signification is all-important to the scene which features Vince and his mirror (he is about to embark on a date with a man a bit older than him who is an accountant).

Text: *Queer as Folk*

HAZEL: Fine, come for tea.

NATHAN: (Stomps out) It's like having two mothers.

JANICE: And whose fault is that –?

Beat, NATHAN gone, JANICE on the edge, HAZEL kind.

HAZEL: Give it time, we'll wear him down. I've banned *EastEnders*, he's livid –

VINCE cuts across, bad mood, stronger than usual (in unpacking the shopping, he hasn't noticed how on edge JANICE is).

VINCE: It's very simple, Janice. You go upstairs, you pack his bags, shove him in the car and take him home! Who's in charge, you or him?

Stopped in his tracks by JANICE, suddenly in tears, HAZEL looking daggers.

JANICE: He says London. Every time I try, he says London. And he *could*. Plenty boys his age just take off – (Breaks off, upset)

HAZEL: He likes it here too much. While he's here, he's safe.

JANICE: I just don't know *why*. What have I done wrong?

HAZEL: He's fifteen, that's all. First time in his life, he gets to be centre-stage. Happens all over, Janice, some boys don't come out of the closet, they explode.

VINCE: What about his dad, can't he do anything?

JANICE: He won't talk about it. (Pause. Quiet;) Won't talk at all. Not one word. (Pause. Then all the anger breaks out) I can't tell *anyone*. If I even tell his *school*. They'd tell social services, they'd have to. And there's Helen, she's ten years old, what happens to her? She gets interviewed? She gets her name on a register, at ten years old?

HAZEL: They won't, love, all they'd do is visit –

JANICE: Oh well *you'd* know, wouldn't you?

Nasty silence.

JANICE (cont.): I'm sorry, I didn't mean to . . . (Bright, artificial smile) Got it wrong, didn't I? Somewhere along the line, I got it all wrong. (to VINCE) He'll be all right though, won't he? I mean, if he's out on Canal Street . . . Keep an eye on him, could you?

VINCE: Course I will.

JANICE: (Still flustered) Thanks, I'd better . . . Thank you.

JANICE goes.

HAZEL: Oh well done, Vincent, reduce a grown woman to tears. Like no one's talked to her till you come blundering in, what's the matter with you?

VINCE: (Feeble) I've got a date.

5/21 INT. VINCE'S BATHROOM, DAY 10 19.30　　　　　　　　**5/21**

VINCE

VINCE in the mirror, brushing his teeth, looking at himself, despairing.
CUT TO – VINCE, plucking nostril hairs with tweezers.
CUT TO – VINCE, using a cotton bud to get gunk out of the corner of his eyes.
CUT TO – VINCE, doing his hair, all gelled flat.
CUT TO – VINCE, doing his hair, gelled all spiky.

CUT TO – VINCE, showering his hair.
CUT TO – VINCE, doing his hair. As normal.

5/22 INT. VINCE'S BEDROOM, DAY 10 19.40   5/22

VINCE

VINCE, in a full-length mirror, trying on a shirt. He tries to get a good look at his arse, doesn't like what he sees.
CUT TO – VINCE, in a different shirt.
CUT TO – VINCE, in yet another different shirt.
CUT TO – VINCE, in a suit.
CUT TO – VINCE, in the original outfit, unhappy, trying out the line:

VINCE: No, I don't want a pension. Cameron, just stop right there. No pension. No.

5/23 EXT. RESTAURANT, NIGHT 10 19.59   5/23

VINCE

VINCE, approaching the restaurant, on his mobile.

VINCE: It's all your fault. If I end up with life insurance and endowment policies and stocks and shares and things, you're paying for it, all right? Where are you, anyway?

**5/24 EXT. CANAL STREET, INTERCUT WITH EXT.
RESTAURANT, NIGHT 10 19.59**   5/24

STUART, MARTIN/VINCE

STUART on his mobile, MARTIN at his side.

STUART: We're going to Via Fossa, I've got a new friend, his name's Martin. So you won't be missed.

Commentary

This script shows how dialogue is combined with camera instructions. We cannot analyse the meanings of the language used in this example without considering accompanying visual signification. Indeed, the context in which these utterances are made is crucial. For example, the meaning of the lines

VINCE: It's very simple Janice. You go upstairs, you pack his bags, shove him in the car and take him home! Who's in charge, you or him?

depends on us knowing whether or not the speaker has a concerned expression on his face, whether he is smiling, and where he is positioned in relation

29

to Janice (does he have his arm around her?). Here, the shooting script tells us how the visual signification will work when filmed:

> *Vince cuts across, bad mood, stronger than usual (in unpacking the shopping, he hasn't noticed how on edge Janice is).*

The script also makes it clear that some scenes are heavily dependent on visual meaning, possibly with no dialogue at all. We understand that Vince's scene in front of the mirror is about the dilemma of what to wear on a date – there are no lines of dialogue which explain this, but a quick succession of shots does the same job even more effectively.

CONNOTATION

At a first level, signifiers denote things. As with the example of the rose, the word or picture denotes the flower. **Denotation** is the literal or dictionary meaning of the signifier. There is, though, a second level of meaning attached to the sign 'rose'. In English culture roses are also about romance (a dozen red roses means 'I love you') and have other sets of associations, such as the idealised English country garden. Media images of the late Princess Diana often strove to combine these associations and she was referred to as an 'English rose' for her fair looks.

Connotation is about how words or images or sounds have particular meanings and associations within our own culture. It is through connotation that we convey cultural attitudes, beliefs and values. As we have seen, in Western culture roses connote romance but they are used more specifically to signify heterosexual love. The publishers Mills & Boon, for example, use the signifier of a rose on their paperback covers which therefore comes to mean a specifically heterosexual romance. Dominant connotations of the word 'romance' still invoke a notion of young, heterosexual couples – from Romeo and Juliet to Victoria and David Beckham.

Connotations carry social judgements. We can say that signs carry positive and negative connotations. For example, the signs 'bachelor' and 'spinster' at a level of denotation simply mean an unmarried man or woman. The connotations of each have been historically different, however, demonstrating the kinds of social judgements that signs carry. The word bachelor has historically connoted carefree young males with a desirable lifestyle. The word spinster carried far more negative connotations, evoking images of old, 'unfulfilled' women having been 'left on the shelf'. These differences explain why spinster is seldom used today except in specific contexts such as the marriage ceremony, but it is interesting to note that, without the word spinster, there is no female equivalent of the term bachelor, except for the recently invented US term 'bachelorette'.

Activity

Analyse the example of a print ad in Text: Advertisement. First, break down the signs in the text into signifiers and signifieds, remembering that you can apply this to any word or image there might be in the ad. At this level you are investigating denotation. Now move on to identify the connotations of the same signifiers.

Text: Advertisement

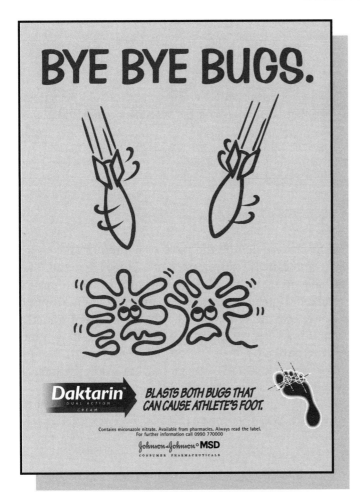

31

Commentary

This advertisement of a treatment for the skin disease 'athletes' foot' consists of arbitrary and iconic signifiers. At the level of denotation you may have recognised the following elements: the written language consists of arbitrary signifiers that give information about the product: its brand name (Daktarin), what it can do, and the company that produces it (Johnson & Johnson). The visual images denote a foot, germs and missiles. However, it is clear that, to understand how the ad works as a whole to bestow on the product positive connotations, we have to recognise the associated connotations attached to all these signs. Johnson & Johnson have chosen to use a light-hearted approach rather than a scientific one to sell this product. The connotative meaning of the word 'blasts' and the images of missiles function as symbols of the product and its power to destroy germs quickly. The artist's impression of the germs connotes them as alien and ugly and therefore things that justify expulsion via 'warfare'.

Extension

Collect a selection of television advertisements (it would help to videotape them). Analyse them, distinguishing between denotation and connotation.

METAPHOR

Signs, as we have seen, can be the parts of written or spoken language, such as words, and can also be images or non-language sounds like music. These signs have different kinds of relationships to the things and ideas that they represent or refer to; they don't always represent things directly. A word or image may be used symbolically, to represent something else entirely, something with which it has certain features in common. This is known as **metaphor**.

The most explicit kinds of metaphor are similes, which acknowledge the comparison of one thing with another:

My love is like a red, red rose

He had a face like a stopped clock

But metaphors are also expressed without this acknowledgement, as in these examples:

1 'Heart of Glass' (Blondie)

2 'Piece of my Heart' (Shaggy Feat. Marsha)

3 'Sowing the Seeds of Love' (Tears for Fears)

These three examples of song titles are typical of metaphors used in popular music. Many songs are about being in love or being hurt by lovers, so certain metaphors turn up again and again. One of the most common is the use of the heart as a metaphor for the emotions, as in the phrase 'a broken heart'. Also commonly used are metaphors for love and sex which use notions of the elements to represent passion. The properties of fire (consuming, dangerous) or storms (disruptive, destructive) and rain (tears, or having the power to wash things away) parallel some of the properties of passionate relationships, evoking intensity of feeling.

Images are often used metaphorically in film or television texts. A character knocking a wineglass over and spilling red wine onto a white cloth might be used as a metaphor for the start of a feud or war, or for the loss of sexual innocence. Curtains opened to allow sunlight to stream into a room could signify the restoration of hope, or happiness.

Activity

Find examples of song, book, film or television programme titles which use metaphor.

(Note: there is no commentary on this activity.)

METONYMY

A word or image may also signify something in a condensed or 'short-hand' way, for example by representing only a part of something to refer to the whole. This kind of reference is known as a **metonym**.

A metonym is useful, for reasons of economy, when it can stand in memorably for a complex set of values. When James Bond orders his trademark martini 'shaken not stirred', the drink is a metonym for his glamorous lifestyle, and also communicates his self-confidence and understanding of 'good taste' or class distinction.

Metonymy is also often used narratively. When, in the book *Dracula* (1897), the hero and heroine are attacked by a vampire, this, it can be argued, represents what were, in Victorian England, a range of social, sexual and cultural threats. Another example would be the use of a particular incident as a metonym for a more complex, ongoing situation, such as when the men in the British film *The Full Monty* (1997) start dancing in line at the jobcentre. This is a metonym for their whole journey from unemployed steelworkers to male strippers, which has now given them back some self-respect.

Advertising tends to use stereotypical images of people metonymically. The young couple walking down the aisle of a supermarket, or enjoying a holiday in the sun, are metonyms for a whole range of people who fall into similar broad social categories.

Metaphor and metonymy are not only used in fiction. An example of how they might be used in non-fiction can be found in television documentary where, for instance, the focus might be on the story of one person, so that a young man talking about his heroin addiction and his everyday life on a deprived estate is a metonym for other addicts and also for the whole 'social problem' of drug use amongst young men, particularly on estates where there is poverty and unemployment. A documentary maker might also use metaphorical images: a recurring example occurring at the ends of news documentaries is the use of shots of interview subjects walking by the sea shore or a river, with a voice-over. This is used to suggest a sense of aftermath, reflection or tranquillity.

Activity

Look at a selection of this week's newspapers and find examples of photo-journalism, or other pictures used to illustrate stories. Note as many examples as you can where an image, or set of images, is used to signify things or ideas metonymically. A typical instance of this would be a photo of a single, hungry, crying child who is used to represent a whole famine. This is effective because it personalises a large-scale, impersonal phenomenon for us.

(Note: there is no commentary on this activity.)

METAPHOR AND METONYMY COMBINED

Many shots, speeches, scenes and narratives in television texts are both metaphorical, in that they represent something else, and metonymical, in that they are a condensation, or shorthand version, of something. The most obvious examples can be found in sequences which have to convey a variety of meanings quickly, such as trailers and titles.

One example is the opening titles of *Coronation Street*. The bird's-eye view shots of chimneys and rooftops serve both as a metaphor for community and 'community values' and as a metonym of a thousand other ordinary streets, the streets and communities in which we, the viewers, might well live. The name 'Coronation Street' metonymically represents a set of values connected with post-war Britain, defined by relatively stable social classes and a centralised national identity.

Another instance is the TV-advertising figure of the 'caring, capable mum' who has come to replace the older advertising stereotype of 'the housewife'. She is often represented as going to work as well as being a mother, but her great concern is still her children. This figure is a metonym of working mothers who might buy the convenience products advertised, such as washing tablets or ready meals. When this 'mum' (a typical advertising designation) is shown washing her little boy's football kit in fabric conditioner or dishing up chicken kievs for the family, this is metonymical of her caring for her children, and also a metaphor for the feelings (warm, protective, nurturing) she is meant to have for them.

35

Activity

Watch and make notes on an episode of a soap opera. Look for and identify examples of metaphor and metonymy in particular scenes. You could consider any or all of the following:

◎ dialogue or other language
◎ imagery
◎ narrative.

(Note: there is no commentary on this activity.)

MEANING IN TELEVISION TEXTS

Using the theory of semiotics and looking at different kinds of signification, this unit has been exploring meaning. We have seen that, not only do linguistic signifiers, like written or spoken words, work to create meaning, but that images and non-linguistic sounds do too. In this way, images can function in a similar way to language.

We must take account of the fact that language in television is usually meant to be understood in conjunction with images. Our location of meaning in a television text is dependent on visual signifiers and non-linguistic sound, like music, in interaction with language. It must also be remembered that language on television is usually spoken, whether as dramatic dialogue, informative direct address, or 'chat'.

In every television text, then, signification is complex. There are particular features of signification which characterise different kinds of television texts. For instance, domestic dramas tend to use more close-up camera shots. This is because these dramas are concerned with relationships between people and the close-up is a conventional way of signifying intimacy, human feelings and the details of non-verbal communication.

Television advertising generally relies on striking visual imagery, colour and music to get the audience's attention and to take advantage of the connotations of words, images and sounds in a very short space of time. It produces a swift succession of images like beautiful people, sunlight, dripping golden butter and speeding red cars, and sounds such as birdsong, fast dance music or soothing classical strings.

In a typical scene from a television quiz show, we can see that its meaning relies on images and sound as well as language. We make meanings from visual cues; for instance we watch the close-ups as the camera lingers on the contestant's face or nervous hand movements, or on the question master's expression, in order to fully engage with each moment and to read the way in which the game is moving. The set is also a visual realisation of what the contest is about. In the UK programme *Who Wants To Be A Millionaire?*, for instance, the contestant sits in a chair opposite the host of the show, with two consoles or desks between them. The positions have connotations of an interrogation or interview, an impression heightened by lighting the contestant with a single spotlight at the point where the questions get harder and the amount of money on offer increases. Sound cues feature at this point also, as the music swells dramatically, signalling a rise in tension.

The quiz show also locates meaning in its narrative, which is the 'rags to riches' story of an ordinary person acquiring money by skill or luck, not over a lifetime but in an hour.

Meaning also comes from the language of the show, for example at the level of cooperative dialogue between the contestant and the host. The question master in *Millionaire* asks a series of questions and deliberately delays his own confirmation of the answers given by the contestant. The question master is the initiator and ultimate controller of the conversation.

In *Millionaire*, language is also meaningful at other levels. A type of language which values knowledge, judgement and cognitive skills, as we do in the arena of education, is used: contestants are told that questions will 'test their knowledge' and they are congratulated for 'good deduction'. However, another type of language here seems to contradict the first: contestants are said to be 'winning' or 'losing'; they 'stake' or 'bet' the money they have already won; and they get 'lucky' over their answers. This type of language relates to gambling, where chance, not skill or knowledge, is important.

Activity

Videotape, or watch and make notes on, a programme which takes place in a studio with a host. This can be anything from a dating show like *Blind Date* (UK) to the National Lottery programmes (these types of shows are often broadcast on Saturday evenings).

Analyse the text you have chosen in terms of how language, visuals and music all work together to produce meanings.

(Note: there is no commentary on this activity.)

Extension

Complete the above activity working in a small group. Collect several examples, then write them up and present your joint analyses to your class or seminar group.

SUMMARY

This unit has introduced the theory of semiotics, which explains how images and sounds are able to make meaning, as signifiers, in a similar way to language. It has demonstrated that linguistic features, such as connotation, metaphor and metonymy apply also to signifiers like still or moving pictures or music. It makes the point that, in a television text, language is always understood in conjunction with these other kinds of signifiers, combining with them to produce meaning.

three

Forms of television

This unit explores ways in which the meanings of television texts for readers/viewers depend partly on generic classifications and related structural factors such as narratives, themes and character functions.

The unit will go on to examine the negotiations of meaning between television texts and readers.

GENRES

Genre comes from the French word meaning 'type' or 'kind'. In English the word is used in an academic context in the study of textual media, such as film, painting, literary fiction, music or television.

To describe a text as belonging to a particular genre is to classify it by type. Texts are grouped together in genres when they have, or seem to have, characteristics in common. We can therefore refer to film genres, music genres, fiction genres or television genres. Genres are therefore groups of texts which share conventions.

An example of a film genre is 'the gangster film'. Historically, many films have used a dominant theme of the criminal activities of (usually) American male gangsters or Mafia members; classic examples are *The Godfather* (1972) and *Goodfellas* (1990). Specific examples of twentieth-century popular music genres are jazz, soul, indie rock and speed garage.

This classification of texts is not scientific, however. It is difficult to say who decides what genre a text belongs to. Texts may not even be easily categorised into one genre. Texts are generally categorised by a consensus negotiated between different groups. These include the creative industries, such as film and television makers; broadcasters and distributors; cultural critics like 'arts' reviewers in magazines and news-papers; and the readers and audiences of popular fiction, film, music and television.

It is important to remember, therefore, that genres and the names given to them are not fixed. It is perhaps more important to be able to describe the features that groups of texts share than to try to 'fit' texts into 'correct' genres. However, it is also important to remember that textual genres are highly meaningful and are significant structuring factors for the content and reading of texts.

Activity

Study Text: Best-sellers and identify the language used to let potential readers know what to expect from these books. What genres are explicitly mentioned?

(Note: there is no commentary on this activity.)

Text: Best-sellers

Data supplied by Whitaker BookTrack from the Total Consumer Market period w/e 7 July 2001

	Title	Author	ISBN	Publisher	RRP	Comments
HARDBACK FICTION						
1	One for My Baby	Parsons, Tony	0002261820	HarperCollins	15.99	Heartbroken language teacher returns to London to find the world he knew, changed
2	How to be Good	Hornby, Nick	0670888230	Viking	16.99	Doctor's husband gives up cynicism for good works
3	Thief of Time	Pratchett, Terry	0385601883	Doubleday	16.99	Race to stop the only clock in Discworld
4	Warlock	Smith, Wilbur	0333761340	Macmillan, London	18.99	Black arts needed to save Egyptian dynasty
5	The Watchman	Ryan, Chris	0712684166	Century Pub Co	15.99	A duel to the death between an SAS soldier and the man who trained him
6	A Traitor to Memory	George, Elizabeth	0340767073	Hodder	16.99	Violinist loses all musical memory except the weeping of a woman and a single name: Sonia
7	P is for Peril	Grafton, Sue	0333741463	Macmillan, London	10.00	Detective follows trail of missing doctor
8	On Green Dolphin Street	Faulks, Sebastian	0091802105	Hutchinson	16.99	Washington affair leads to cold-war intrigue
9	Seven Up	Evanovich, Janet	0747269564	Headline Bk Pub	10.00	Bounty hunter is dropped into a smorgasbord of murder, kidnapping and extortion
10	The Fourth Hand	Irving, John	0747554323	Bloomsbury Pub	16.99	A man loses his hand but his search to become whole again soon makes him realise that it takes more than a new limb to find fulfilment
HARDBACK NON-FICTION – GENERAL						
1	The Lost Boy	Pelzer, Dave	0752838709	Orion	12.99	Memoir of life in care
2	Diana: Story of a Princess	Clayton & Craig	0340770805	Hodder	18.99	Myth vs reality
3	Man Named Dave	Pelzer, Dave	0752841149	Orion	12.99	Abused child finds himself
4	Marie Antoinette	Fraser, Antonia	0297819089	Weidenfeld & Nicolson	25.00	Flaunting, extravagant queen – or was she?
5	Madonna: An Intimate Biography	Taraborrelli, J Randy	028307289X	Sigdwick & Jackson	16.99	Queen of Pop under the microscope
6	The Map That Changed the World	Winchester, Simon	0670884073	Viking	12.99	William Smith, the founding father of geology
7	Dazzler: The Autobiography	Gough, Darren	0718144686	M Joseph	16.99	Life story of Yorkshire and England bowler

	Title	Author	ISBN	Publisher	RRP	Comments
8	Henry VIII: King and Court	Weir, Alison	0224060228	Cape	20.00	Find out how much the gardener was paid
9	Help Yourself	Pelzer, Dave	0007114796	Thorsons	9.99	Lessons of a tough life shared
10	War Diaries, 1939–1945	Alanbrooke, Viscount	0297607316	Weidenfeld & Nicolson	25.00	Long awaited memoirs of WWII

HARDBACK NON-FICTION – REFERENCE

	Title	Author	ISBN	Publisher	RRP	Comments
1	Nigella Bites	Lawson, Nigella	0701172878	Chatto	20.00	Quick and easy
2	Return of the Naked Chef	Oliver, Jamie	0718144392	M Joseph	20.00	More basic cooking
3	House Doctor Quick Fixes	Maurice, Ann	0007122403	HarperCollins	14.99	House looking boring? Buy this book
4	Eat to Beat Arthritis	Patten & Ewin	0007116195	HarperCollins	9.99	A diet to aid mobility
5	Delia's How to Cook: Bk. 2	Smith, Delia	056338431X	BBC	16.99	Second part of learning-to-cook trilogy

PAPERBACK FICTION

	Title	Author	ISBN	Publisher	RRP	Comments
1	Roses are Red	Patterson, James	0747266999	Headline Feature	6.99	Alex Cross up against a bank robbing mastermind
2	Bridget Jones's Diary (combined)	Fielding, Helen	0330375253	Picador	6.99	Sex and the single girl
3	Sushi for Beginners	Keyes, Marian	0140271813	Penguin	6.99	Trials for 3 Dublin women
4	Last Precinct	Cornwell, Patricia	0751525359	Warner	6.99	Scarpetta finds herself framed
5	Captain Corelli's Mandolin (film tie-in)	Bernieres, Louis De	0099422042	Vintage	6.99	WWII romance in Aegean Sea
6	Man and Boy	Parsons, Tony	0006512135	HarperCollins	6.99	Media career crumbles
7	The Holiday	James, Erica	0752843303	Orion	5.99	Romance on Corfu
8	Bridget Jones: The Edge of Reason	Fielding, Helen	0330367358	Picador	6.99	More sex and the single girl
9	White Teeth	Smith, Zadie	0140276335	Penguin	6.99	
10	Chocolat (combined)	Harris, Joanne	0552998486	Black Swan	6.99	Chocolate vs Church

CHILDREN'S

	Title	Author	ISBN	Publisher	RRP	Comments
1	Harry Potter and the Goblet of Fire	Rowling, J K	0747550999	Bloomsbury Pub	6.99	Harry faces his biggest test yet
2	Harry Potter and the Philosopher's Stone	Rowling, J K	0747532745	Bloomsbury Pub	5.99	Harry discovers his past

	Title	Author	ISBN	Publisher	RRP	Comments
3	Harry Potter and the Prisoner of Azkaban	Rowling, J K	0747546290	Bloomsbury Pub	5.99	Harry meets his Godfather
4	Harry Potter and the Chamber of Secrets	Rowling, J K	0747538484	Bloomsbury Pub	5.99	Harry talks to snakes
5	Fantastic Beasts and Where to Find Them: Comic Relief Edition	Scamander, Newt	0747554668	Obscurus Books	2.50	Harry's text book

PAPERBACK NON-FICTION – GENERAL

	Title	Author	ISBN	Publisher	RRP	Comments
1	A Child Called 'It'	Pelzer, Dave	0752837508	Orion	5.99	Abused by an alcoholic mother
2	Bad Blood: A Memoir	Sage, Lorna	1841150436	Fourth Estate	6.99	Frank account of parents' secrets
3	McCarthy's Bar: A Journey of Discovery in Ireland	McCarthy, Pete	0340766050	Sceptre	6.99	Looking for the Ireland of childhood holidays
4	Extra Virgin	Hawes, Annie	0140294236	Penguin	6.99	Writer and sister move to Italy
5	Kitchen Confidential	Bourdain, Anthony	0747553556	Bloomsbury Pub	7.99	Behind the scenes in restaurants
6	Is it Me?	Wogan, Terry	0563534222	BBC	6.99	The Togmeister tells all
7	Olive Farm: A Memoir of Life, Love and Olive Oil	Drinkwater, Carol	0349114749	Abacus	7.99	Farm restoration in Provence
8	Elizabeth	Starkey, David	0099286572	Vintage	7.99	The greatest monarch of them all
9	The Bodyguard's Story	Rees-Jones & Johnston	075153126X	Warner	6.99	The last drive
10	Snake Oil	Diamond, John	0099428334	Vintage	7.99	Does alternative medicine work?

PAPERBACK NON-FICTION – REFERENCE

	Title	Author	ISBN	Publisher	RRP	Comments
1	Dr. Atkins' New Diet Revolution	Atkins, Robert C	0091867835	Vermilion	6.99	A new way to eat
2	Official Theory Test for Car Drivers and Motorcyclists	Driving Standards Agency	0115521186	Stationery Office Books	11.99	All you need to know
3	The Naked Chef	Oliver, Jamie	0140277811	Penguin	12.99	Cooking stripped bare
4	Driving Theory Test Questions	British School of Motoring	0753505606	Virgin Books	5.99	All you need to know
5	Proms Guide: 2001		0563534338	BBC	4.50	If music be the food of love . . .

Extension

Visit a multiplex cinema and study film posters and preview trailers, or obtain a film magazine which previews forthcoming films.

- ◎ What genres of films would you describe them as?
- ◎ What other films are they like?
- ◎ What kinds of audiences do you think might go to see the different film genres?

TELEVISION GENRES

Traditionally, the texts in television schedules fall into broad generic categories which guide programme makers and viewers. Main generic categories are drama, comedy, light entertainment, arts, documentary, news and current affairs.

Drama is a broad genre usually classified into more specific sub-genres, such as:

◎ **Classic, single play or literary drama**

Dramas described like this are usually either dramatic adaptations of literary novels, for example Jane Austen's *Pride and Prejudice*, or are written as single plays, whether for the theatre or specifically for television. They are prestigious forms seen as 'authored' in the same way that novels are authored. UK television playwrights who have been historically influential are Dennis Potter, who wrote *The Singing Detective* and Alan Bleasdale who wrote *The Boys From the Blackstuff*.

◎ **Detective and police drama**

These two genres are interconnected and both deal, in different ways, with the defining of social deviance and the processes of law enforcement. Detective dramas tend to centre on a lone, often eccentric, detective. His (or more recently, her) job is to discover – where others fail – how, why and by whom a crime has been committed and to bring the criminal to justice. Police dramas on the other hand feature an ensemble of characters, usually ordinary working police officers of all ranks who are based in a police station. Working as a team, they deal with and resolve a variety of more mundane crimes and disorderly incidents, as well as spectacular crimes.

◎ **Domestic drama and soap opera**

Domestic dramas centre on the home, the community, the workplace and, in particular, are concerned with interpersonal relationships such as those between lovers, family members or groups of friends. Some domestic dramas, like *Cold Feet* (UK), which centres on three young professional couples, are prime time one-offs or series, but the most ubiquitous form on television is the half-hour serial soap opera. British soaps centre on neighbourhood communities, the families who live in them and their everyday lives. They feature ensembles of characters and follow multiple storylines. They are the only television narratives that never end.

Comedy is a broad generic category that includes compèred stand-up, 'live' comedy shows, sketch format shows that feature a series of short comic situations and scenes, such as UK examples *Monty Python*, *French and Saunders* or *The Fast Show*, and situation comedies – sitcoms – like *Friends* (US) or *The Royle Family* (UK). Sitcoms could be classified as half-hour comic dramas but are not usually described as dramas because, conventionally, television drama is not seen as a primarily comic form.

Light entertainment is a generic category that includes game and quiz shows, variety shows featuring a mixture of chat, singers, comedians and speciality acts, and also chat shows like *So Graham Norton* (UK), in which a host talks to, and plays games with, celebrity guests.

Arts programming has tended to mean, by contrast, heavy or seriously-toned broadcasts, such as classical music concerts, theatre productions, ballets and operas.

Documentaries are factual, usually short, films researched and produced to be informative about particular subjects, people or situations.

News bulletins consist of a series of segments which give factual summaries of daily national and international events; they may cover items about Parliament, foreign conflicts, natural disasters or personal stories about well-known people. Current-affairs programmes often have similar political and social content to news bulletins, but will usually be less segmented and will explore the wider issues in more depth, introducing different opinions and interpretations of events. Typical topics could include farming methods, food safety and risks to public health; controversial government policies; and wars and famines in other countries with their underlying causes.

Activity

In a group, study the television programme guide reproduced on p. 6 or choose one day from your own TV guide, and categorise as many programmes as you can into the genres discussed above.

Discuss any problems you have had in categorising the television texts into these genres and try to say why the problems arose.

(Note: there is no commentary on this activity.)

REPETITION AND ORIGINALITY IN GENRES

Generic television texts all contain familiar and new elements. Audiences anticipate the familiar pleasures of known generic conventions. If we like romantic dramas, we expect a narrative in which people are sexually and emotionally attracted to one another, fall in love, or are perhaps tragically prevented from becoming lovers; we anticipate these kinds of themes. However, we do not want a mere copy of previous romantic dramas; we want the story to contain innovative elements – 'twists' – too. We also expect some new kinds of characters, themes and situations as social and cultural attitudes to love and sex change.

Activity

To highlight what we expect and don't expect from a genre, complete the following activity, ideally working in a group. Compose a short child's bedtime story which includes the following:

◎ some conventional, familiar fairy-tale elements

◎ some unconventional, innovative elements, such as new settings or characters or an updated ending.

(Note: there is no commentary on this activity.)

INTERTEXTUALITY, HYBRIDITY AND NEW GENERIC FORMS

As television texts proliferate and audiences become increasingly media-literate, television genres frequently refer to, merge with and develop new forms from existing genres.

Intertextuality

Television genres also often refer to other popular media genres and other television; this is known as **intertextuality**. For example, daytime magazine programmes like *This Morning* ('Richard and Judy', UK) comment on and feature items about and excerpts from other current television shows. They also construct and incorporate features about personalities, actors and issues from other television genres. The American animated sitcom *The Simpsons* makes humorous references to other popular cultural genres like pop music and film.

Comic television genres which rely on parody are always inter-textual, since they are referring to the conventions of 'straight' genres which they recreate in an exaggerated and distorted way. For example, the situation comedies *The Thin Blue Line* (UK) and *Operation Good Guys* (UK) were parodies of police dramas.

Hybridity

Television genres also rapidly hybridise. A **hybrid** is the combined result of two or more original forms and retains some characteristics of those forms. The following texts are examples of hybrid television genres.

The X-Files (US) combined elements from both the detective genre and the genre of science fiction. The central protagonists are FBI agents whose job is to enforce law, and to detect and solve crime. However, the cases which they uncover always involve supernatural or alien forces and causes. Moreover, the aliens often turn out to be conspiring with government agencies like the FBI itself. The programme's popularity was probably due to its encapsulation of a national mood of mistrust of law-enforcers and government combined with an increasing interest in 'new age' subjects like psychic powers and extra-terrestrials.

Buffy the Vampire Slayer hybridises two popular US television genres of the teen high school soap and horror. In *Buffy*, the central protago-nist is a teenage girl who also happens to be a demon-slayer. She and her friends worry about the usual rites of passage of high school like dating, school grades and oppressive adult authority. They also have the responsibility of keeping the town's population of supernatural creatures under control. In this text, the friends' school, Sunnydale High, is quite literally a 'hellmouth' and the anxieties of adolescence are embodied as monsters and demons which have to be fought and defeated.

Activity

Find two or three different programmes which you think are hybrids of other genres. What genres are they hybrids of? Identify what elements in them derive from the original genres.

Commentary

You may have noticed some of the following similarities between documentaries and soaps. Like a documentary, the characters in the UK programmes *Airport* and *Children's Hospital* are not actors but real people and the programmes invite us to look at the real world where events are actually happening rather than the world of fiction. In soaps we have little sense of mediation but, as in documentary, we are much more aware of the presence of the production team in *Airport*. However, like soaps, *Airport* is about the everyday lives of a number of ordinary people and their interpersonal relationships.

New generic forms

As television culture changes, new generic television forms develop. They may be created in response to an expansion in broadcasting. For instance, breakfast television was developed when broadcasters realised people were prepared to watch in the early morning. Increasing need to fill more broadcasting hours cheaply has led to shows like *Police, Camera, Action* (UK) and *When Animals Attack* (US), which rely mainly on police surveillance camera or amateur camcorder footage. New generic forms also develop as an acknowledgement of changing and narrowing audience categories, for example 'magazine' programming – so called because it is structured like a magazine, with previews of contents and relatively self-contained segments. There have already been magazine programmes for daytime viewers, gay audiences, youth audiences and so on.

New generic dramas develop as both audiences and the societies and cultures they are part of change. In the 1990s, for example, a series of British television dramas developed into two distinct, identifiable generic strands.

One new genre might be called 'thirty-something' drama or modern 'comedies of sexual manners'. They are concerned with the lifestyles, interpersonal relationships, careers and rites of passage anxieties of middle-class young professionals. They include UK dramas such as *This Life*, which concerned the relationships and professional anxieties of a group of young lawyers, *Cold Feet*, *Teachers*, and *Queer As Folk* which is about the work and private lives of young gay men. Some of these dramas are more radical, others are safer; but all tap into a particular Zeitgeist ('spirit of the age') and provide new generic conventions, expectations and pleasures.

Another new generic strand has been a series of female ensemble UK dramas such as *Making Out*, *Band of Gold*, *Real Women*, *Playing the Field* and *Fat Friends*. Their shared characteristics are that they feature mixed groups of women, usually friends and/or co-workers, and the narratives centre on their personal, work and family relationships. Key themes are the importance of female friendships, the differences between women and the ability of women to relate to each other as a team. Their narratives assume a 'female' point of view. It is interesting that both these new generic drama strands are concerned with gender, changing gender relations and both masculine and feminine identities.

Activity

Identify a new genre which has emerged on television in recent months or years and discuss its main characteristics. Consider, for instance, 'reality TV' phenomena like *Big Brother* (UK), *Castaway* (UK) and *Survivor* (UK and US).

(Note: there is no commentary on this activity.)

STRUCTURES AND CONVENTIONS IN TELEVISION GENRES

Narrative

Unit Two explained how narratives are organised through certain codes and conventions that enable us to recognise their movement through time and space. In popular television genres, the most familiar narratives are constructed as movement from **equilibrium** to **disequilibrium** to a **new equilibrium**. That is, an initial situation is disrupted, giving rise to drama or humour, until a new equilibrium is restored in the ending, usually through the resolution of problems or complications that were the cause of the disruption.

Traditional narrative structure is **linear**, which means that a series of events is arranged in chronological order. For the creators of genres, this involves selecting where a narrative begins and ends and choosing which events to include and which to omit. Linear narrative often follows the actions of a central protagonist, usually the hero with whom we are encouraged to identify or sympathise. Identification and sympathy may be achieved by constructing the narrative from the selective point of view of this character.

However, we cannot assume that all television texts will be structured in this way. One of the most interesting genres in terms of narrative is soap opera. Soaps offer multiple storylines which run simultaneously and, because they are continuous or endless series, they do not have conclusions. Instead, soaps contain temporary resolutions or endings to storylines. For example, the UK *EastEnders* soap character Mark Fowler, who is HIV+, found that his illness was brought under control when he tried new drugs. This was a resolution of the immediate problem, but we knew at that point that Mark was not 'cured' and that he would face problems with his illness in the future. Because soaps are constructed around multiple storylines, there is no central hero who carries the action, drives the narrative forward or represents a dominant point of view. Instead, we are offered the opportunity to sympathise, disapprove of, or identify with, many different characters through narratives of their everyday lives.

Activity

Watch or videotape an episode of a soap opera such as *Coronation Street*, *Emmerdale*, *Family Affairs* (UK) or *Hollyoaks* (UK) and work out how many storylines appear in that episode and how they relate to one another to produce a complex picture of that soap's particular world.

(Note: there is no commentary on this activity.)

Setting and situation

An important element of meaning in television texts is setting. We expect city streets for police and crime dramas; brightly coloured studios and flashing lights for game shows; a news desk and TV monitors for news broadcasts. Television texts also rely on recurring situations. In soaps we can anticipate that someone from a regular character's past will often return. In quiz shows, the final competitor has to answer all the questions under pressure and without mistakes to win the big prize. In news broadcasts the presenter will always introduce and conclude the bulletin, but will also regularly hand over to an outside broadcast 'on the spot' reporter or conduct a live interview with someone in the studio. All these are familiar settings and situations.

Themes

All generic texts have consistent dominant themes. In the popular television medical drama, for instance, the dominant theme is the resolution of crises by medical personnel such as doctors. This has spawned many similar dramas, which might be called emergency-services dramas, in which doctors, nurses, paramedics and firefighters form the central teams who deal with and resolve crises; not only medical emergencies and burning buildings, but also the personal problems of the people they come to help. These dramas have become at least as popular as police dramas in recent years, possibly suggesting that emergency-services personnel are now important figures of moral authority. The resolution of both practical and personal emergencies in these dramas is desired and expected by their audiences. These themes are part of the conventional pleasures of the genre.

Characters

Genres rely on stock characters such as the male detective and his sidekick in crime dramas, or the young female 'hostess' in game shows who brings on the contestants and the prizes. Characters are important to narrative because they tend to serve particular functions. If we look at the classic detective genre we would notice that the narrative often follows a male central character – the detective – who is accompanied by a male sidekick. UK television detectives *Inspector Morse* and *Frost*, for instance, are both loners, whose special powers of deduction are superior to those of the other characters in the text, including the entire police force. On the other hand, the sidekick, e.g. Sergeant Lewis in *Inspector Morse*, is more ordinary and likeable. He has a social life and may be married or romantically involved. Crucially, he is always one step behind the brilliant detective. Part of the sidekick's function is to represent us, the ordinary viewers, who cannot see what the detective can see and must wait for him to solve and explain the crime. Female characters in detective stories historically occupied marginal roles either as victims of crime or as romantic figures who dangerously distracted the detective-hero from the proper business of solving crime. Since dramas like US TV's *Cagney and Lacey*, which featured two female police detectives, and Granada's *Prime Suspect*, in which a female detective headed a murder squad, more women detectives have emerged as heroines.

Characters are crucial to dramas, but we can also say that news stories, wildlife documentaries and docusoaps rely on characters whose narratives we follow, whether those characters are politicians, meerkats, air hostesses or the villain 'Nasty Nick' from *Big Brother*.

Activity

Choose two of the following television genre narrative options and reconstruct Text: Pig farmers opposite as part of a script for the appropriate generic forms:

◎   a television evening news bulletin

◎   a scene from a soap opera

◎   a scene from a police drama.

Take into account the following factors:

◎   narrative form

◎   point of view

◎   dialogue.

(Note: there is no commentary on this activity.)

Pig farmers get the boot

FARMERS A. AND B.____ – the men blamed for the national foot-and-mouth crisis – were evicted from their pig farm for breaching safety guidelines, it emerged today. And an exclusion zone has been thrown around the farm at a major tourist attraction because of the foot-and-mouth scare.

School parties will be turned away from the farm this week following action by environmental health officers. But as the incineration of animal carcasses got under way around the country, the *Gazette* has discovered that the local Council had the ____ brothers ejected from ____ Piggeries seven years ago for keeping pigs in squalid conditions.

The brothers, who now live in a different area, fought the case for two years before they were evicted after an agricultural land tribunal.

Last week it emerged that their leased farm was at the centre of the national foot-and-mouth epidemic after they sold allegedly infected livestock to other farms.

Today the mass incineration of thousands of animal carcasses was under way as the foot-and-mouth outbreak continued to spread.

(The *Shields Gazette*
26 February, 2001)

The structures of meaning and conventions of genres mentioned so far carry with them particular views of the world which also imply social and cultural values, attitudes and judgements. Genres may provide familiar pleasures to confirm our world views or may reassure us by symbolically resolving social problems which cannot actually be solved. The changes and innovations which constantly occur in generic forms may, however, challenge our world views and 'common-sense' notions.

TELEVISION AS A GENERIC MEDIUM

Television, as a popular mass medium, is also a generic medium. It is dependent on texts – programmes – which can be easily categorised into recognisable types. This is partly because television is a domestic medium and texts are viewed as part of audiences' everyday lives.

Television is also a commercial medium, meaning that its audience is also its market – texts are the products it sells to its audience. All television channels and companies compete for viewers in order to justify the money they receive either from advertisers and sponsors or from the government in licence fees.

Generic texts are therefore crucial to television's commercial success. Generic programmes are already familiar, categorised and structured and so can be more quickly planned, created and broadcast in order to satisfy television's huge demand for texts. Generic texts also provide vital predictability in that viewers are able to anticipate types of programmes they enjoy because of previous experience. For the television companies, a genre which has already proved successful with particular audiences will be used to create new texts within the same, or a similar, genre in hopes of further commercial success.

Generic texts are now increasingly important in delivering niche audiences. Advertisers carefully choose advertising slots around types of television texts whose predicted audiences most closely correspond to the people advertisers want to sell particular products to. Advertisers and programme makers therefore expect specific types of people to watch and engage with specific genres of television texts.

Activity

Look at the commercial breaks during a youth-oriented soap such as *Hollyoaks*, *As If* (UK) or *Dawson's Creek* (US).

- What kinds of products are being advertised?
- What types of people would you expect to buy these products? Think of factors like age, gender and lifestyle.
- Does this profile correspond to the types of viewers you would expect to watch the programme?

(Note: there is no commentary on this activity.)

Generic elements and meaning

Genre also structures cable and digital television production and viewing to the extent that some channels are, in effect, 'genre channels', broadcasting 24-hour comedy, news or sport; or they provide a series of texts that are generically very similar to one another, for example home decor and gardening programmes.

The recurrence of generic elements means we derive pleasure from expectation and prediction. For example, in the UK soap *EastEnders* we know heartache is in store for Dot Cotton when her son, 'Nasty Nick', turns up; or in a medical drama such as *Casualty*, we can predict when a situation is bound to lead to a medical emergency. These expectations also mean that we know what types of programme we will be watching when we select our evening's viewing, because we are already familiar with their conventions and codes. However, it does not follow that the meanings we derive from a text are determined by these generic elements, or that a television text consists of one 'true' meaning. To gain a deeper understanding of how meaning is produced when we watch a television programme, it is necessary to consider in more depth the role of the audience.

Television texts as polysemic

Television programmes are characterised by **polysemy** which means that a text has potentially many meanings. For example, every episode of the UK soap *EastEnders* is comprised not of a single set but of a multiple set of meanings.

A major storyline in the year 2000 raised the issue of teenage pregnancy when a 15-year-old schoolgirl, Sonia, became pregnant after a one-night stand with a young man, Martin Fowler. One potential meaning relates to Sonia's boyfriend, Jamie, and his response to Sonia's pregnancy when he angrily tells her she is a 'slag'. Here the text draws attention to negative connotations about young women, even though we are aware that these connotations contradict what we know about Sonia. Nevertheless, it implies that the sexual behaviour of young women needs to be monitored. Since there is no direct male equivalent of a 'slag', females in our culture are in a unique situation in relation to certain values that the audience of *EastEnders* understands as common sense. Sonia is a 'good girl' who made a 'mistake' and is not a 'slag', and yet she can only be defined as 'good' in relation to dominant values, whereby females are judged more harshly than males in regard to sexual activity.

55

The concept of polysemy is important because it implies that meanings are not imposed on an audience, they are **preferred**. In other words, a text has many meanings but we can examine it to identify a preferred meaning. In the *EastEnders* example, Sonia is the focal character because she is both a 'good girl' and a schoolgirl mum. The meaning of her character is ambiguous, but according to the narrative we know she is not a 'slag' and so the text is structured in such a way that we are more likely to sympathise with her and less likely to agree with Jamie's outburst. However, this does not mean that all viewers will disagree with Jamie's judgement.

DOMINANT, NEGOTIATED AND OPPOSITIONAL READINGS

Texts reproduce and at the same time reinforce cultural ideas, which in turn govern how men and women should behave. Television advertisements reproduce dominant Western cultural values. Consider, for example, the many advertisements for household products. In these, women rather than men are most likely to be seen doing the housework for their (usually) appreciative husbands and children. These advertisements draw upon cultural codes that represent male and female differences and work to reinforce such gender differences as normal and natural. Even when texts do depict a man using household products such as kitchen cleaner, the assumption is that this man is performing women's work for a very specific reason, such as to get praise for temporarily standing in for the woman.

However, viewing television advertisements and programmes like *EastEnders* is an active process that involves making sense of, or **decoding** the text so that it becomes meaningful to us. A prominent theorist in media studies, Stuart Hall (1980), explained that messages are not 'simply transmitted', they are produced (a process known as **encoding**) by the makers of the text and then decoded by the audience. The audience is not an undifferentiated mass, but consists of individuals who belong to distinct social groups according to their age, class, gender, ethnicity, sexuality and so on.

Hall developed a way of understanding how different people construct different meanings from the same television text. He proposed that there are three possible positions from which we can decode a text. The first is the **dominant reading** position, whereby the viewer takes the meaning of a programme in a way that is harmonious with the way in which it has been encoded. For example, we may watch a respectful news item about the royal family uncritically, accepting its assumption that they are a valuable British institution.

The second decoding position is the **negotiated reading** position, which involves negotiating between the viewpoint encoded in the text and a viewpoint which differs somewhat. For example, while watching the news coverage of the royal family we may agree with the programme's assumption that the monarchy is a good institution for Britain on the whole, whilst simultaneously believing that the privileged class position which royalty represents does not promote equality for all groups in society.

The third decoding position is the **oppositional reading** position. According to Hall, this is the position occupied by the viewer who is aware of the dominant encoded position, but who elects to decode within an 'alternative frame of reference'. This corresponds to the position of the anti-royalist viewer who listens to a news report on the royal family and feels that society would be better off without them altogether.

If we return to the *EastEnders* storyline about Sonia's pregnancy, we can say that the text could be interpreted in three ways. The audience could reproduce the preferred meaning and reject Jamie's attack on Sonia as unjustified or even sexist. Alternatively, the audience could produce a negotiated reading: they may reject Jamie's point of view that Sonia is a 'slag' and accept the preferred meaning, while simultaneously believing that teenage pregnancy is the cause of many social problems. An oppositional reading would be to understand the text's assumption that the two-parent family is an 'ideal' family while rejecting or challenging those same values.

There are, of course, other possible readings of this storyline, but Hall's model highlights the ways in which a text's structure limits the meanings that are possible, while at the same time accounting for diversity in the meanings that may be produced by the audience.

Activity

As a group, watch a videotaped or live television news bulletin. Construct the possible dominant, negotiated and oppositional reading positions in one news item.

(Note: there is no commentary on this activity.)

SOCIAL READERS

Social factors such as our age, gender, ethnicity, class and sexuality influence how we read a text such as *EastEnders*. In the 1980s, a researcher in media studies, Dorothy Hobson (1982), carried out a series of interviews with people who were avid viewers of the popular UK soap *Crossroads* and published the results in a book entitled *Crossroads: The drama of a soap opera*. Hobson wanted to find out why the programme was so popular as well as what the viewers disliked about it.

Hobson found that, to make meaning, viewers used their own experiences to relate to the social issues raised in the soap. She also discovered that the context in which a television programme is watched is important. To watch a programme with the mother of young children, she said, is a very different experience to watching with an elderly person who lives alone. Family situation, she continues, is vital to both our ability to view with attention and also the way in which we relate to a programme. Hobson's research has been very influential because it clarified the ways in which meaning is not a one-way process. Rather, the contribution of viewers to a television programme is as important as what programme makers put into it.

Another researcher, David Morley, who published *Family Television: Cultural power and domestic leisure* in 1986, also studied the consumption of television by interviewing families in their own homes. His research demonstrates how watching television involves social relations as much as it involves interpretation of individual programmes. For example, he found that husbands tend to dominate when it comes to programme choices and are more likely to have control of the remote. (Interestingly, this aspect of family politics has been used as the source of humour in the sitcom *The Royle Family*.) Further, women were more likely than men to choose fictional programmes, such as soaps, as their favourite genres, whereas men said they preferred non-fictional genres such as news broadcasts and sports programmes. Similarly, women said that they talk about soaps and the issues raised in them with their friends, but men said that they never talked about fictional programmes with their friends.

What is important about such research is that it has highlighted gender as a factor that influences the way in which we respond to television texts. Other studies have shown that social class, age and ethnicity are further factors. For example, a middle-aged woman may share her teenage daughter's love of soaps such as *EastEnders*, but there may be marked differences as well as similarities in their responses to specific episodes, which could be partly explained by the age difference between mother and daughter.

Watch an episode of *Coronation Street* or another popular soap with a group of people, perhaps with fellow students or at home. Afterwards, carry out a discussion as to your most and least favourite male and female characters.

How might some of the different viewpoints about the characters within your group relate to factors such as the viewer's age, gender or ethnicity?

(Note: there is no commentary on this activity.)

SUMMARY

This unit has introduced the generic aspects of television texts and explained how their conventional structural elements relate to their meanings and interpretation. It has also further extended the notion of how meanings in television texts are not fixed, but are open to a range of readings which are influenced by social and cultural positions and values.

Unit four

'Live' talk

This unit examines the use of 'talk' on television in the context of exchanges or conversations, e.g. between television presenters and other participants. It also looks at some features of speech, like the distribution of different accents and dialects notable on television.

TELEVISION AND SPOKEN LANGUAGE

The language of the television landscape is largely spoken. Written language rarely appears, the major exception being the optional addition of subtitling for the hearing-impaired. Even this conforms to the patterns of verbal communication in that it is informal and impermanent. It is also speech represented in writing, rather than writing as communication. Television is a medium organised around the rhythms of speech, not writing, and around accompanying visual signification such as the gesture, appearance and demeanour of speakers.

Units four and five deal with the primary examples of spoken discourse (i.e. spoken language-in-use) on television. Discourse is further defined here as language-use, as communication and interaction between people.

The two main forms of 'talk' in television texts are:

◎ dialogues, monologues and narrative voice-overs in dramatic forms of television such as one-off dramas, soaps or sitcoms
◎ scripted or spontaneous 'talk' in non-dramatic forms of television such as news, documentary, 'magazine' programmes and other 'factual' programming.

We refer here to this second kind of talk as 'live' talk to distinguish it from represented talk such as that in dramas. However, that does not mean that the programming referred to in this unit is all broadcast 'live', although some of it, such as news bulletins or studio magazine programming like Saturday morning children's TV or breakfast TV, is a combination of live and pre-recorded features.

This 'live' talk can take the form of direct address to the viewer, as when a newsreader reads the news to 'us' or when a presenter welcomes us back to a breakfast programme after a break. It may also take the form of commentary, as when viewers 'overhear' a sports presenter describing the events at an athletics meeting, or when we listen to a voice-over on a nature documentary. Live talk also often takes the form of conversation, which ranges from the formal political interview to 'chat' between presenters and celebrity guests or members of the public.

THE 'VOICES' OF TELEVISION

Television is presented to the audience by figures who are, in effect, the 'voices' of the medium. These television presenters fulfil various functions. They are the authoritative voices who read the news and anchor the film reports given by journalists outside the studio. Presenters also investigate – as journalists on our behalf – on hard current affairs programmes like the BBC's *Panorama*, or on softer consumer advice programmes. Presenters are the 'hosts' of celebrity chat shows and act as compères or masters of ceremonies for game shows and 'live' comedy shows, i.e. they introduce, oversee and direct their 'guests' and what happens during the show. Presenters also maintain continuity or cohesion for viewers between and across programmes: 'And in half an hour it's *The Holiday Show*, right after *Emmerdale* . . .', or 'Join us on tomorrow's programme when we'll be talking live in the studio to the detective in charge of the case.'

Another level of **mediating** voices, so called because they interpret for us and relay things to us, are those who fulfil regular and occasional expert roles which could range from a familiar 'TV chef' to an academic or other professional invited onto a current affairs programme to give an expert view of something in the news. There are also many performers on 'live' television, such as comedians, singers or personalities who may also appear in host or presenting roles themselves, such as the comedians who perform to a studio audience, but who also have guests and other performers on their shows. Some host-performers interact with others outside the studio world, such as presenter Mark Thomas, who subjects politicians and prestigious figures to comic humiliation in his political journalistic investigations, and Graham Norton who accesses web sites and makes phone calls to members of the public during filming of his chat show.

Members of the public or 'ordinary' people constitute a further layer of figures and 'voices' who appear on television. They are visible most usually as the audiences for studio-bound game shows, chat shows and sitcoms, providing responses which aim to correspond to those of the wider audiences watching at home. Ordinary people also appear as guests on magazine shows as themselves, for instance as people who have gone through a traumatic experience with which the audience can identify, or as models to be given makeovers. They may also appear on magazine or current affairs programmes, as campaigners who are attempting to get the law changed for instance, or because they are involved in the news of the day and can speak about these events from a personal or 'personal-political' point of view. Ordinary people are also the amateurs given a chance to take part in quiz shows, or to become audience-participants who provide entertainment in game shows and certain kinds of chat show. Their appearances are regulated by the presenters and hosts who control the direction of the programme.

Activity

Look back to the TV guide reproduced in Unit one, or look at a current TV guide. Discuss what mixtures of presenters and other people appear in the kinds of TV genre which feature 'live' talk. Discuss the various roles these people have in different programmes.

(Note: there is no commentary on this activity.)

SPEAKING ON TELEVISION

One of the main features of live television is the presence of a person (or persons) speaking directly to camera and therefore to us, the audience. This **mode of address** can make for compelling viewing because it is as though that person is actually talking to us. For example, evening news broadcasts usually feature a formally-dressed newsreader, often in a suit, who delivers a scripted commentary in the form of **direct address**. Camera shots are either close-ups or medium shots with little camera movement and virtually no cuts unless to go over to another reporter. Everything about a newsreader's body language, or non-verbal communication, stresses their sincerity and authority. For example, arm movements are kept to a minimum and eye contact with the camera is maintained throughout because it signifies honesty.

The conventions of the direct address depend upon the genre or type of television text. The conventions in news broadcasting can be used as a parody and for humorous effect in programmes such as the UK's *They Think It's All Over*, certain advertisements and satirical television programmes. In programmes such as these, their relative informality dictates different conventions. Gestures, for example, will be less restrained and facial expressions will be more animated.

Situational variation also dictates the mode of address, such as formal or informal address, which changes from one kind of television text to another. Different non-dramatic television texts talk to their audience in various ways according to the context. Presenters of a 'magazine' genre programme or chat show, for instance, will use the intimate first person 'I' and address the audience as 'you', as though they are known by the audience as friends: 'I don't know about you but I'm dying to find out who won the Brit award for best newcomer'.

Activity

Watch a range of 'live' talk television programmes and note what different modes of address are used and in what kinds of situations.

Discuss whether you think there are particular people on television who most typically use direct address to the camera/audience. Do you think this mode of address can give these people authority? If so, what kind of authority?

(Note: there is no commentary on this activity.)

CONVERSATION

Interactive talk on 'live' programming takes the form of conversation between those taking a presenting or hosting role and others. It is public conversation which is always designed to be 'overheard' by the television audience.

As with all conversation, this broadcast form has conventions which guide the participants as to the direction it will take and the boundaries it has to observe, such as what can be said and what cannot. However, these conventions are not the same as those which govern spontaneous private conversations. A current-affairs presenter knows the boundaries of the questions it is possible to ask a government minister before offence is incurred, but any offence is rarely personal; rather it is that a representative of government objects to a journalist having overstepped the line of an unspoken agreement between government and the news media with which it cooperates.

In the first of the following two examples, a news and current affairs presenter has a three-way conversation with representatives of relevant organisations in the form of an interview. In the second, a daytime television presenter talks with a TV chef who appears on her programme. The analysis examines the conventions these conversations observe, their direction and purpose and the different roles of the participants in terms of controlling, negotiating and competing in the conversation, as well as the common ground between them. Also analysed are the intent, purpose and apparent effect of individual contributions to the conversations and the strategies employed by the speakers.

Current affairs interview/one

On an evening news programme, a news presenter (NP) interviews the president of a national organisation for farmers (PF) on video-link and, in the studio, the political director of an animal welfare organisation (AW).

The studio set in this segment visually represents the positions of the speakers in the conversation: NP, the presenter, is seated behind a desk, with one 'guest' to her left and the other, on a video-link screen, to her right. If she faces forwards (to camera) NP is addressing us, the audience. If she turns left or right, this allows her to determine which of the other participants should contribute to the conversation. The news studio set is formal and relatively bare except for the desk and electronic equipment, and the participants are also quite formally dressed in suit jackets. Both suggest a work-like atmosphere.

NP, as presenter, effectively determines where this 'conversation' begins and ends. She first acknowledges the audience to the interview, emphasising that it is for their benefit; then the participants are given titles (they are not just 'themselves') which also function to designate their roles or positions in this public conversation – PF and AW are there to represent the views of their respective organisations, and NP is there to control and anchor the conversation:

> NP: Well I'm joined now by PF [she gives his title and position] and AW [she also gives his title and position].

Throughout, NP determines where participants enter the interview, as she does after the introductions, when she nominates PF to speak:

> NP: First of all, PF, we heard from the chief vet there [referring to a previous news report] that hundreds of farms are under investigation.

There is already **common ground** between the participants, not personally but as media professionals or representatives and speakers in the political public sphere. NP goes on to establish further common ground in the context of a national outbreak of disease amongst livestock and of what has happened so far. This acknowledgement of 'what we already know' is indicated by the word 'presumably'. Also, however, she is indirectly asking the first speaker questions which require answers. She has also indirectly supplied his answers by making assumptions about what he is going to say:

> NP: That presumably means there are bad times ahead for Devon farmers in the next two or three days (1) presumably you will identify other outbreaks in your area.

PF treats these observations as questions when he answers 'Yeah', but his answers supply further information which confirms the statements NP has already made by assumption:

> PF: Yeah (.) I'm afraid we're staring into the abyss at the moment in the south-west (.) we know there are a lot of other farms under observation and the ministry are expecting to find other cases of foot and mouth disease (.) the nightmare scenario, if you like, is we get it on Dartmoor.

By using different language than is required to minimally give the information about the situation, such as referring to a metaphorical 'abyss' and a 'nightmare scenario', PF is also conveying his attitudes and feelings – or those of the members of his organisation – to the situation. When we talk, we are actually doing so to achieve something in the wider world. PF makes factual statements which describe the situation, but which also make an emotional statement appealing for recognition of the situation as his members will see it.

The overall shape of this interview is governed both by the time and topic constraints which are ultimately determined by the broadcasting organisation, in the person of NP, and by the **agendas** – the predetermined sets of objectives – of the three participants. PF is at one point given space by NP to speak directly to the audience and, in particular, to his constituency of farmers in his official role as farmers' adviser:

NP: You are (.) as it were a point of help and advice for farmers (1) what are some of (.) almost (.) the everyday, small things they're worried about?

PF: One of the most frequent queries we've had is how do I recognise foot and mouth in my sheep (.) because people know the classic symptoms in cattle but it's not so common in sheep (.) we are appealing to farmers who've got sheep to be very (.) very vigilant.

NP gives him this space partly because, in such a context, the BBC news is seen to have a 'public service' role in giving information as well as in investigating the situation. This is consistent with NP's agenda, as is her elicitation of the 'everyday, small' details that will humanise the situation for viewers.

NP primarily shapes the conversation by nominating the **turn-taking** of speakers, by limiting their contributions and by directing them with a series of questions they must answer. NP wishes to introduce the issue of whether the foot-and-mouth disease outbreak has been partly the fault of modern farming practices and so redirects PF in his turn to speak:

NP: But presumably the transport of animals is so much greater now (.) and the volume of transport (.) there's no question of containment.

PF then defends his position and rejects this suggestion:

PF: If you go back to 1967 [the last major outbreak of the disease]
      cattle and sheep were being moved around the country then (.)

NP, however, wishes to pursue this point and so interrupts PF:

NP: But not (.)

as she turns to her left and nominates AW, whom she knows has a
different position on this issue:

NP: (.) can I just bring in AW here (.) presumably not to the same
      degree as they are being moved in 2001?
AW: No (.) this is a development of the last ten years or so and if
      we're going to avoid this kind of problem in the future we
      need reforms (1) we have to stop these long journeys to
      slaughter.

So NP interrupts participants when she wishes to redirect the
conversation or when she wants to cut a speaker off, but within boundaries of conversational 'politeness'. These boundaries are not those that
the same participants would observe if this were a social conversation,
because they are acting as their 'professional selves' and the political and
journalistic requirements of the conversation take precedence over social
ones. This is reinforced by the lack of **phatic** communication in this
conversation. Phatic utterances, such as obvious comments about the
weather, or a compliment on someone's appearance, are a normal part
of everyday social conversation and are made in order to establish and
maintain relationships between the participants. In this interview conversation, such phatic utterances would disrupt the 'official' roles of the
participants and would divert the conversation from its formal agenda.
Similarly, the paralinguistic features of the conversation, such as gestures,
leaning towards other speakers, or cues of facial expression, are limited.
They are largely determined by the formal studio set-up and are almost
entirely connected to NP designating speakers.

This is also how NP controls the **cohesion** and continuity of the
exchanges. Conversational cohesion is prioritised as part of her agenda
in that she is ensuring this on behalf of the audience; neither is it in her
interests as a broadcaster for the conversation to falter.

A particularly important part of NP's agenda is to do with being
seen, as a journalist and representative of a responsible public broadcaster, to provide a 'balanced' enquiry into the situation, for which two
opposing positions have already been set up: the farmers and the animal

welfare lobby. She is not there to enter the conversation about the subject so much as to regulate it by ensuring that a debate takes place in which the disease outbreak can be described, analysed and connected to wider political issues for the audience from two different perspectives. This somewhat reductive notion of 'balance' cannot, of course, include all the many complex attitudes and experiences that people have regarding issues and events.

The agendas of both 'guest' participants are to represent the points of view of their organisations, to defend those where necessary and to compete with each other's point of view. In this interview, they are prevented from any direct competition, such as arguing with each other, because NP always acts as mediator for each of their contributions. They are not, therefore, so much speaking to one another as to the unseen audience. For this reason, AW returns constantly to a point he has made about stopping the long journeys of animals to slaughter. This kind of repetition of a memorable line about an issue is much used by professional communicators who deal with the media and is known as a 'sound bite'.

At a certain point, which will have been determined by the time and 'balance' needs of the programme, NP formally thanks the participants and turns to face the camera/audience. This effectively ends the 'conversation'.

Current affairs interview/two

A breakfast television presenter (BTP) interviews a television 'celebrity chef' (CC) about the same subject of the, then current, foot-and-mouth outbreak.

The studio set immediately marks the comparative informality of this conversation, in that the presenter interviews her guest in a studio set which resembles a living room with comfy furniture, plants and pictures. The set communicates the more intimate and, above all, domestic way in which the same news issue will be discussed. The presenter sits on a sofa, with her guest on another sofa. Neither is 'facing' the audience, although the presenter can and will address the audience directly because the cameras will move around and enable her to 'face' us.

The common ground of the participants is immediately established and is seemingly quite different from that in interview one, because, although both the participants are media professionals, the presenter brings in her guest as if he were a friend:

BTP: Well (.) joining me now (.) top chef and restaurateur [CC – the presenter gives him his full name].

The presenter nominates his entry to this conversation, however, by immediately calling him by his first name and saying:

BTP: It's good to see you (.) you must be such a very sad man because I know you're a champion and such a promoter of British meat (.) you always have been.

The notion of their informal relationship is emphasised by the para-language of the presenter, who constantly reinforces and encourages the chef's contributions by nodding and attentively leaning forward towards him.

In this very first introduction it is apparent that, in this interview, the emphasis will be on the domestic economic aspects of the foot-and-mouth crisis, and the experience of it rather than the politics of it. BTP's immediate introduction of the notion that CC will be 'a very sad man' also sets the emotional tone of the exchange, allowing the participants to make more emotive speech acts, expressing their feelings, than in the more formal interview. BTP's introduction is also illustrative of the greater number of phatic contributions made in this conversation, despite the usual restrictions of broadcast time, in which the presenter emphasises small social 'bonding' phrases.

Cooperation is also enhanced by the fact that BTP offers far fewer contributions than her guest and these are mainly to reinforce and guide what the guest is saying; nor does she interrupt his contributions. BTP does, in fact, have as much control over this conversation for the benefit of the audience as the first news presenter did, but her control here is far more unobtrusive, giving the exchange the feel of a friendly chat rather than a purposeful interrogation.

BTP leads the conversation by asking the types of questions which are designed to prompt long declarative or instructive statements from her guest rather than defensive answers. He is given the opportunity to air his ideas at length about how the crisis might affect domestic cooking and how viewers can deal with it. It is an important function of his contributions to this conversation to give this advice, since he has been brought on as an expert in this sense.

BTP has the same agenda as the news presenter did, in that she is here to regulate this conversation to the requirements of the TV broadcast, but, because the interview has not been set up in a deliberately oppositional way, but rather as an exploration of the foot-and-mouth crisis from the point of view of its domestic impact on ordinary people, the participants appear to have a shared agenda as to the direction of the conversation and, therefore, no competition or disagreement is apparent.

BTP constantly feeds back short verbal agreements with CC's statements, saying 'you're right' or using similar phrases. This again reinforces an assumption that, not only do the two participants share common ground, but the viewers will also share similar attitudes and beliefs.

CC makes far more emotive speech acts than the guests in the more formal political interview, expressing his particular opinions and feelings about farming and 'Britishness', which he connects together:

> CC: But our farmers have done a great job (.) we're going to have to think about importing meat (.) I know some people are against it (.) you have to consider it (.) it's on the shelves (.) buy it (.) but don't forget the British farmer when the thing turns round again and let's give them lots of support.

Although the presenter picks up on a potentially controversial topic – the import of meat into Britain because of the crisis and the production of cheap meat by factory farming – she represents this as a domestic rather than a 'political' issue:

> BTP: No (.) that's right (.) the thing is though (.) food (.) as you say is either going to (.) we're going to have to think about importing it (.) maybe we're going to have to have a rethink and actually, you know, we have been getting relatively cheap meat, haven't we?
>
> CC: Sure (.) that's right (.) yes (.) I think we've got to be prepared to pay that little bit more (1) but I think we've got to analyse what we're eating ourselves (.) we've got all these cookery programmes on TV (.) it's the big thing of the moment (.) we've become quite complacent.
>
> BTP: Yes.

The viewers are also included here in the same community as the two participants, who emphasise the use of 'us' and 'we' when talking about the domestic effects of the crisis, at the same time making assumptions about a particular version of modern 'family life' being shared by viewers:

> CC: Think about it (.) we need less food in real terms if we sat round the table more, rather than have the mother, the father, then the children eating separately (.) if we all got back to the

table again, with a big pot of (.) bring the neighbours in (.) share with the family next door (.) people will argue (.) we'll all want to eat but the wastage factor will be less, therefore we'll be more economic in what we're doing.

BTP further emphasises the common domestic ground between herself and her audience, which is important to the 'persona' or image of her as a sympathetic daytime presenter, by invoking a shared experience of family life:

BTP: No that's true (.) 'cause some families, it's like a café (.) absolutely (.) someone's sitting there eating beans on toast (.) someone else over there (.) and it's all different times.

BTP finally sums up the smoothly cooperative direction and intimate nature of the conversation/interview when she terminates it in order to introduce the next item:

BTP: I agree with you [she uses his first name] (.) thank you (.) very much indeed.

So in each of the two interviews here, the discussion is quite different, enabled by the different ways in which the presenters control these symbolic conversations according to the agendas of their specific programmes.

Activity

Watch and make notes on, or videotape, a television programme that includes 'live' talk as an exchange, e.g. a news interview, magazine programme or chat show, and analyse:

◎ the main 'conversational' features of the exchange, like cooperation, cohesion and speech acts
◎ the ways in which the agendas of the participants are realised, and particularly the ways in which the presenter controls the 'conversation'.

(Note: there is no commentary on this activity.)

SPOKEN LANGUAGE VARIETIES ON TELEVISION

All the opening moments of texts you have collected will be 'correct' English in the sense that any person who speaks English as their first language will understand them. However, formality and informality in style are often regarded as correct or incorrect use of language. For example, informal style is sometimes perceived as 'bad' language or 'slang' because it is often spoken with a regional **accent** and **dialect**, whereas formal style is more like the dialect that we are taught in school when we learn to write. The term 'accent' refers to the way we pronounce words. We can talk about regional accents when we compare the different ways people pronounce the same words. There are potentially differences in pronunciation between, say, a person from London and a person from Liverpool. In Britain there is one accent, though, that is not located regionally. This is called Received Pronunciation, or RP, although it is not used by a majority of people. Traditionally it was used – and still is used – by those who come from the middle and upper middle social classes, and especially from 'educated' social backgrounds. It therefore carries with it social prestige and some authority, although we can say that this is changing to some extent as British society changes.

In the UK Saturday morning programme *SM:TV Live*, the presenters Ant and Dec are from Newcastle and Cat is from London. Dec could read the same script as Cat but, because they are from different parts of Britain, they would pronounce the words differently. Dialect refers to something else. The term dialect describes the varying vocabulary and grammar used by groups of people. Thus, if we compared Dec's use of words such as 'Haway man give us me hat back, me mam gave us it!' with Cat's form 'come on guys gimme my hat back, my mum gave it me!', we would be discussing dialect.

There is an important difference between regional dialects and Standard English dialect. The latter is spoken by some groups of people and it is the dialect that we are taught to use at school and encouraged to use when we write essays. It is also regarded as a model of 'good' English and it is the dialect taught to people studying English as a second language. Therefore, it tends to be regarded as the norm from which regional dialects deviate. However, sociolinguists have shown through research into both the history of English and its current variations, that all dialects are equally complex, rich and communicative in terms of their grammar and vocabulary; i.e. linguistically speaking there is no such thing as an 'inferior' or 'bad' dialect.

Sociolinguists have also identified that characteristics of regional dialects that are commonly regarded as examples of 'bad' English when

73

measured against the standard dialect, such as the double negative 'She ain't got none', have been a part of English for many years and were once a feature of the standard dialect. Yet our responses to the two forms (A) 'She ain't got none' and (B) 'She has none' would probably be that (B) is the correct form. Linguistically speaking, 'correctness' is not a meaningful *description* of different kinds of English, but rather a *prescription* of how to use English that dominant groups, such as those with the power to govern and educate, have imposed on less dominant groups.

The notion of **correctness** is important to any examination of the language of television because it has been such a controversial issue since the medium's early days. Television news is a prime example. In the 1920s radio broadcasts began, and those who were in control of the, then new, medium decided that a non-geographically-defined dialect would be used by newsreaders rather than any from the variety of local dialects, such as the 'Geordie' Newcastle dialect or the 'Scouse' Liverpool dialect, that characterise spoken English. Instead, the non-local dialect, Standard English, spoken with the RP accent became the dialect and accent listeners heard when they tuned in to BBC news on the radio. This combination was referred to as 'BBC English' and this association has lasted throughout the development of television as well as radio. We hear other varieties of English on television but, in order to maintain an appearance of authority and impartiality, the national news still tends to be read in Standard English dialect and in an accent that is a modified version of RP.

Studies on how people regard accents and dialects have shown that the combination of RP and Standard English dialect is still regarded as the spoken language of those who are most intelligent and authoritative.

Activity

Analyse a random sample of 'live' and factual television texts. Assess the types of programming that tend to rely on modified RP and Standard English speakers, and the types of programming that use speakers with regional accents and dialects.

Commentary

Since RP and Standard English are the accent and dialect associated with authority and power, you will have found that it is most likely to be used by newsreaders, and for voice-overs in current affairs programmes and documentaries. On the other hand, regional accents and dialects will be used in less 'serious' texts. There is, though, a trend towards regional accents in more serious programmes, albeit using Standard English. For example, prime time news presenters may have distinctive Welsh or Scots accents. We are more likely to hear regional accents on specifically regional programmes, like local news round-ups, which help give these kinds of programmes a 'local' identity. We hear presenters with a variety of regional accents on other television programmes, but we less often hear non-standard dialects being spoken.

As well as the social and regional variation of accents and dialects, speech changes according to our membership of other social groups. For instance, it will change if we speak English as part of a minority ethnic group, or of a subcultural group, such as schoolchildren or youth followers of particular music and styles of dressing.

Activity

Think about different ways in which your own speech changes, not only as a result of the context of conversation, but as part of the social group you are currently with. You can, for example, compare the speech you use in college when speaking with different people like friends or lecturers, or the speech you use with your family or at work. Do you find this kind of social speech variation on television? If so, where?

Commentary

Changes in your speech might include degrees of formality of address; different conversational cooperation or levels of politeness; an emphasis or de-emphasis of your regional dialect; or more or less use of taboo phrases.

Extension

Monitor some television programmes which extensively use presenters and see what patterns you can identify in the distributions of accents and dialects you hear used.

Represented talk

This unit examines the functions of represented talk and the processes of its construction – what can be called 'real life' in television texts. The unit also analyses representation of women's talk, and then explores the concept of 'gossip' as it relates to soap opera.

DEFINING REPRESENTED TALK

One of the main forms of talk on television is represented talk. This is defined here as scripted dialogue which is performed by actors who utter the words in character. It is used primarily in drama, but is also used in representations of actual events in such genres as documentary drama. For example, the BBC investigative series *Crimewatch* contains dramatised accounts of real events which use actors and represented talk, rather than real people and actual talk, to transmit a version of those events.

Of course, represented talk in dramatic songs and plays pre-dates television by thousands of years. The use of represented talk has also always been a feature of prose fiction when, for example, the author uses quotation marks to signal that the text contained within them is meant to be the actual speech of the character rather than the voice of the story's narrator. Such represented talk has also often featured a variety of social dialects.

REPRESENTED TALK AND NARRATIVE PURPOSE

It is important that we are always aware that represented talk can never be a faithful or accurate reflection of actual conversation. When we are watching a television text that contains represented speech, such as a soap or a drama, we are offered a coherence and significance that is not necessarily a characteristic of actual conversation in the wider social world. Even the most mundane conversation between two characters in a soap opera will have a narrative purpose. It may be to establish atmosphere, or so that the viewers can predict what is going to happen in the future, or it may be there for characterisation. In short, the only reason that characters talk to one another in television texts is so that the viewer can listen to them; not, as in real conversation, so that they can listen to each other.

Activity

Consider the possible reasons why the seemingly ordinary exchange between two characters may in Text: *Eastenders* be significant to a viewer.

Text: *EastEnders*

DOT: It's freezing today. I hope the weather improves soon.

PAULINE: Yes, it was lovely yesterday wasn't it?

The significance of this dialogue is entirely dependent on situation and context. It may be to establish an atmosphere of 'normality' – the impression that the Queen Vic is a place where friends can meet and exchange utterances that are similar to the conversations we have in real life. On the other hand, its significance might be to provoke prediction or invoke a sense of danger – the viewer may be aware that Pauline's teenage son has stolen a car and is driving fast through country lanes. Represented talk has to be relevant to narrative and characterisation, so it is not simply a reflection of real talk.

SCRIPTED CONVERSATION AS REAL CONVERSATION

When we watch television dramas and sitcoms, voyeurism, or the impression that we are unobserved while eavesdropping on private conversations, is constructed through the representation of real talk. Its effect is that it appears not to be written or that it is unscripted. The UK television sitcom *The Royle Family* derives its humour through its reference to the everyday speech of an 'ordinary' family living in Manchester. The family consists of a woman called Barbara, her husband Jim and their children Anthony, who is sixteen, and Denise, who is twenty-six. The following is a dialogue from this sitcom:

> BARBARA: Bill has loads of money.
> JIM: Mmm.
> BARBARA: He bought a sliced white.
> JIM: What are you telling me that for?

This exchange between the characters is humorous because it draws attention to the kind of irrelevant statements we sometimes make in response to other people's utterances in real life. However, we rarely hear irrelevant conversation in texts and, indeed, the writers of *The Royle Family* have used this aspect of real talk for very specific reasons. First, it is used to establish the atmosphere of *The Royle Family* as one in which nothing much seems to be happening. It is also used for characterisation and it is also important to narrative.

Despite the impression that nothing is happening, *The Royle Family* is in fact a story. In the first episode, for example, we learn from the family's talk about their money, relationships, occupations and leisure activities, much about them as people. It establishes that Barbara is about to go back to work part-time at the local bakery and that Denise is soon to be married to Dave. We also learn that Jim and Barbara are a couple who tend to stick to traditional gender roles within the confines of the home: Barbara does all the cooking and housework for the family, while Jim worries about money and paying for Denise's wedding. Although they all enjoy watching television, Jim watches it most attentively (he spends less time getting up and down, or in the kitchen where there is no television set, than the other characters) and it is he who tends to manage the remote control.

By the end of the series the narrative has moved through time and the characters have developed. We go through the ups and downs of Denise and Dave's relationship that culminates in their marriage; Barbara is established in her job at the bakery; and sixteen-year-old Anthony has acquired a girlfriend. In other words, the conversation performs the dual functions of character development and moving the narrative forward.

In *The Royle Family* what is established in every episode is that watching television in the living room together is very much a part of this family's everyday domestic routine. Conversation, or rather, the kinds of conversation they have are the source of humour in the text.

A specific example of talk itself as a theme of *The Royle Family* can be found in Episode one of the first series screened in 1999. Jim, who is sitting in his chair, which faces the television, is examining the family's telephone bill. Repeating the script of a television advertisement for BT he shakes his head:

JIM: Ninety-eight quid! It's good to talk my arse!

This first episode of *The Royle Family* in which a father grumbles about the cost of telephone conversations, complains about electric lights being switched on and the expense of his daughter's forthcoming wedding, serves to establish the ordinary family situation within which the narrative develops. The function of the script is to represent an ordinary family's conversations and the viewer is expected to find humour in it. It is within the framework of this apparently ordinary, trivial talk that the narrative develops.

Conversation is a cooperative type of talk in which two or more people engage in a form of turn-taking. In real life, silences can create embarrassment because they are signs that everyone involved is searching for something to say and that the conversation has failed in some way.

In scripted talk it is rare to construct silence unless the aim is to produce an atmosphere of tension. *The Royle Family*, however, features those comfortable periods of silences that do occur in conversations between people who live together or who know each other very well. Similarly, instead of looking at one another when they talk, the characters often fix their gaze on the television screen, which means that the topic of conversation is frequently turned to the programme they are watching. However, even the seemingly 'typical' conversation featured in the sitcom *The Royle Family* cannot be described as a straightforward reflection of real speech.

Real conversation is characterised by spontaneity. Although in many circumstances we will mentally rehearse or prepare what we want to say to people and how we want to say it, most of our encounters with people cannot be planned with any precision or in any detail. To do this we would need to be certain of how others are going react to what we say and what they are going to say to us, whether or not they will interrupt, and so on. Conversation involves deciding what we want to say as we speak, and this can result in a large number of **hesitation markers** such as 'er' and 'em', which fill the pauses that occur before we have finished speaking: 'I bought my tickets from, er, the student travel shop.' We also spend time **backtracking** when we repair our sentences: 'I picked them up last Wednesday – no, I picked them up on Thursday.' Sometimes, when we need to repair our utterances, others will assist us by **interrupting**, as in the following:

A: I picked them up last Wednesday, and then . . .
B: Last Wednesday? The travel shop is closed on a Wednesday.
A: . . . sorry. Yes, that's right, it was Thursday.

Interruption is a common characteristic of real conversation, but it is not always used to make a correction or ask for clarification. Indeed, it has a variety of functions. If, for example, we are stuck in a conversation that bores us, we may interrupt rather than say directly that we are no longer interested. Similarly, we might interrupt if the other speaker is dominating the conversation, or conversely, if we are intent on dominating it.

Interruption is thus a kind of overlap, but short overlaps are not necessarily classed as interruptions. The term **interjection** refers to examples of short overlaps in speech. These are not classed as interruptions because they do not stop the flow of the speaker. Examples of interjection include **minimal responses**, such as 'mm' and 'yes', which signal agreement and encouragement, or exclamations such as 'never!'.

Interjections fulfil a supportive linguistic function because they signal to the speaker 'yes, I am interested in what you are saying'. In other words, they provide important **feedback** to the speaker. Because feedback is important, we also frequently use expressions such as 'you know' and 'you see', which indicate the speaker's desire to know that they have the listener's attention.

If these linguistic features are not apparent in another person's speech, we may be suspicious of their sincerity and it can give the impression that their speech is rehearsed. Actors, on the other hand, can only try to replicate such spontaneity. They are rarely given the opportunity to improvise or use their own words and gestures. Usually all of these are prescribed as can be seen in the text below, which is an extract from *The Royle Family*.

Activity

Examine the short script extract in Text: *The Royle Family*. To what extent does the extract replicate spontaneous speech?

Text: *The Royle Family*

MARY: I'll pop in the baker's tomorrow, see how you're getting on. Mind you I'm expecting a big discount.
THEY ALL LAUGH.
JIM: How much is a cup of tea in your bakery?
BARBARA: They don't do tea.
JIM: Same as here then. No chance of drowning.
BARBARA: (TAKING THE HINT) Will you be stopping for a brew, Mary?
MARY: No, I've got a pile of ironing and it won't do itself will it?
MARY AND BARBARA LAUGH AGAIN AS MARY EXITS.
ALL: See ya.
PAUSE.
MARY: Bye.
JIM: She's hilarious, Mary. How does she come up with them?
BARBARA: Come on, Denise, test us some more.

Commentary

The talk is interrupted by scripted entrances and exits that the characters are seen responding to as though it was all happening spontaneously. However, you may have noticed that, unlike real conversation, the characters rarely interrupt one another, interject, backtrack or hesitate.

Extension

Observe and record a real conversation between family members. List examples of interruptions, interjections, minimal responses, hesitation markers and backtracking. Discuss it and compare it with *The Royle Family* or conversation extracted from any other television sitcom or drama.

REALISM

If a television text were to draw attention to the fact that what we are watching is a construction or representation of talk, it would disrupt the impression that we are eavesdropping on a real private conversation. This illusion of the real is referred to in media studies as **realism**. Often our evaluation of a television programme as enjoyable or not resides in its capacity to represent our perception of the real. But realism is a cultural construct and its appearance of naturalness stems from its relationship to the codes, or the 'language of television' as a mode, that give the impression of reality.

On the one hand, the meaning of 'family' in *The Royle Family*, relates to the meaning of 'family' in the wider social world and to our own experiences, but, on the other hand, the representation of family in the programme will be different to our own experiences of family. For example, although the series is set in the real time of its production, that is the late 1990s, the implied viewer will recognise that the value system presented refers to a notion of the past, when households owned only one television set and family members sat in the living room to watch an evening's programming together.

The realism constructed in *The Royle Family* also relates to other television texts and is in many aspects specific to the genre: we understand its representation of family in terms of other representations of family in television sitcom and even in terms of fly-on-the-wall documentary dramas, one of the earliest of which on British television, *The Family*, was an account of the everyday life of an 'ordinary' family.

Realist codes

Realist codes are the signifying processes that programme makers use that refer to our understanding of the real world. The term 'code' is used here to mean a system of signification that works like a language (see Unit two for more information about signification). Realist codes on television can be seen, for example, in the ***mise en scène***. The term *mise en scène* refers to everything the camera reveals in a scene. In the case of *The Royle Family*, it refers to every detail that has gone into the construction of the family living room – furniture, wallcoverings, ornaments, utensils, and so on. These different items are all related realist codes in the sense that they carry the same connotations of class, taste, age and ethnicity that are so important to the realism of the programme. Imagine, for example, changing the comfortable couch that takes centre stage on the set to one made of chrome and black leather.

Realist codes are also seen in individual characters through their speech, clothes and gestures. In *The Royle Family*, the characters all talk in a seemingly authentic regional accent, rather than in a middle-class accent. They talk about certain topics and articulate certain beliefs and values. Similarly, they wear clothes that connote their ordinariness. Jim wears the clothes of a working-class man – worn-out T-shirt and jeans. His unsociable habits, such as picking his nose and scratching his backside, signify his disregard of 'manners' and also his self-confidence within the context of the family home to behave in ways that would be less acceptable in public.

The armchair in which he always sits is very significant because it serves to identify him as a traditional father, and it is important to his characterisation that none of the other family members uses it and that he never sits on the couch. The humour derived from Jim's speech, appearance and behaviour lies, at least in part, in the programme's departure from other popular programmes, such as *ER* (US), that construct a central character who is middle class and physically attractive. On the other hand, Jim's dress is constrained by the same conventions as in real life: unemployed men of Jim's social class would not usually wear a suit and tie when sitting in the house.

Even the most subtle realist code can be made visible by simply taking one element of a programme, such as one within the *mise en scène*, and substituting it with something else. It is then possible to analyse the effect of this change on the realism of the programme. So, if the couch in the Royles' living room was from IKEA or Barbara wore a tweed jacket and skirt, we would probably be critical of the programme's realism or its aim to construct an illusion of the real.

Activity

Identify the realist codes in a recent episode of any popular television drama or sitcom. What kind of change to the realism of the text is produced by altering the *mise en scène* and/or the speech of the characters?

(Note: there is no commentary on this activity.)

Cultural realism and genre realism

Different genres use different realist codes. For example, the realist codes in UK school dramas such as *Grange Hill*, are drawn from **cultural realism**. This means that they are drawn from cultural values and beliefs stemming from what we hear and read about actual young people and schools in other media artefacts such as newspapers, television news or current affairs programmes. However, the US horror programme *Buffy the Vampire Slayer*, even though it too is set within a school, draws more heavily on **fictional realism**. This means that *Buffy* refers more to what we know about the rules of a fictional world, as it relates to the horror genre. This allows the programme the freedom to transgress the boundaries of cultural realism and construct a world that is inhabited with supernatural creatures. We don't comprehend *Buffy*'s conversations about vampire slayers and evil curses in terms of cultural realism but in terms of fictional realism. Nevertheless, even *Buffy* is constrained by the conventions of cultural realism to make the world of high school appear like a world that we recognise. We have to be convinced that, even though monsters lurk in its basement, in all other respects *Buffy*'s school is as real as the school in *Grange Hill*.

It is important to be aware that both cultural realism and fictional realism are constructs. Any appearance of naturalness stems from a text's relationship to the codes – the 'languages' – of television that give a particular impression of reality.

8 5

Activity

Watch an episode of either a medical drama such as *Casualty*, *A&E*, or *Holby City*, or an episode from a science-fiction series such as *Star Trek*, and analyse the way the construction of realism in the programme relates to both cultural realism and genre realism.

(Note: there is no commentary on this activity.)

Production practices and realism

Television texts are the result of other production practices which produce the illusion that what we are watching on the screen is a natural reflection of the real world. In other words, production techniques, such as camera, lighting and sound, work in ways that conceal the processes of their production. Actors, when replicating spontaneous talk between two or more people, never look at the camera. To do this would be to acknowledge the camera's presence and would force the viewer into awareness of the fact that this is represented talk. This is not to say that viewers believe that represented talk is real, rather, that the enjoyment of drama to a certain extent resides in the text's ability to offer the viewer an illusion of reality.

Not acknowledging the presence of the camera is an example of the conventions of realism as it relates to the language of television. Sometimes, though, a text deliberately disturbs this illusion of reality. In the BBC drama *Hearts and Bones* the viewer is given access to the characters' thoughts through the use of voice-over; the US programme *Ally McBeal* contains moments of surrealism; and, in the British teenage drama series *As If*, the main characters frequently talk directly to the camera.

Usually we are encouraged to forget that what we are watching is mediated via a camera, but occasionally programme makers transgress the practice of concealing the apparatus. In the television drama series about the lives of a group of young lawyers, *This Life*, the hand-held camera technique was used to film conversations between the characters. This technique gives the impression that the camera is merely following events as they unfold, in the same way that news reporters sometimes follow participants when they stumble on an event.

This play with the conventions of realism works because television viewers are sophisticated readers of television texts and understand that

86

certain conventions are being subverted in these instances. Because of the ways realist conventions are played with in such texts, they are often evaluated by media critics and viewers as innovative and progressive. What gradually happens then is that notions of realism change to incorporate these innovations, which then become another form of conventional realism. Television drama now does not have to look like a documentary to seem 'real'.

Activity

Television texts often deliberately go against the conventions of realism in order to be innovative and such playing is an essential part of genres like comedy. In terms of talk, characters may break realist codes by speaking to camera, or we may be able to 'hear' a character's thoughts. Characters may break genre boundaries of realism in speech, as in the well-known example of the UK drama *The Singing Detective*, in which characters would begin to sing as if in a musical, although the drama was, in other respects, a realist drama according to, then current, conventions. Can you think of specific current examples?

(Note: there is no commentary on this activity.)

WOMEN'S REPRESENTED TALK

Historically, represented talk on television has been male-dominated. Although there are signs that women's voices are now more likely to be heard on television, since the 1970s much has been written about the prevalence of male voices. The medium has tended to deny women the opportunity to talk, and this can be linked to the wider social world in which women have not had the same rights to speak as men. A notable exception to the absence of women in represented talk is the soap opera genre. British soaps like *EastEnders*, *Coronation Street* and *Brookside*, have been described in the past by media studies researchers as female forms. This is partly because of the ways in which soaps, more than any other genre, focus on the lives of a community consisting of strong, outspoken, female characters of different age groups. Second, the setting is often the domestic or private space associated with women, rather than the public world of employment, money or power. Finally, it has also been regarded as a female genre because it is more concerned with talk or '**gossip**' than so-called masculine genres, which focus on action rather than dialogue.

Gossip

With regard to speech, historically society has judged women's voices as inferior to men's. For example, there are many derogatory words that relate to women's use of language, such as 'gossip', 'nag' and 'chatter', whilst men's speech has been differentiated as 'talk'. Such cultural values and beliefs about men's and women's speech in the wider social world and the tendency to deride women's language-use are often articulated in represented talk on television.

In an episode of the soap *EastEnders* broadcast in March 2001, the character, Phil Mitchell, enters a fish and chip shop where his two enemies Mark Fowler and Ian Beale are in conversation. Venomously he accuses them:

PHIL: You're like two old women gossiping.

The notion that women talk a lot is also used in television advertisements, but not always with the same meaning that the term 'gossip' implies. For example, in a series of BT advertisements in the late 1990s, the actor Bob Hoskins observes different women using the telephone. Through use of direct address, he says to the viewer 'It's good to talk', implying that women are good communicators. The notion that women use language in a different way to men is seen as a fact by BT who use this supposed characteristic of female speech to sell their product.

However, the *EastEnders* example of represented talk illustrates how the term 'gossip' is a label often used to refer to women's conversations and their use of language. The word gossip carries negative connotations about women as talking too much and on certain topics that are connected to the private, emotional world of relationships and its associated spheres of scandals and dramas. But the term 'gossip' has been re-evaluated and ascribed a different set of connotations by feminist linguists who have researched and written on women's use of language.

When linguists use the term 'gossip' in this context it is to refer to the idea that the kinds of conversation women have relate to women perceiving themselves as a group who share common experiences within culture.

Jennifer Coates (1986) researched talk in a group that consisted only of women, who she said, 'met as women'. She found that, although the group talked about many topics, the emphasis was on relationships and emotions.

Coates says that women, when in female company, are more open than are men in expressing their feelings.

Coates is very clear that she is not suggesting that women only ever talk as women. She says women also talk as, for example, students, teenagers, members of ethnic groups, and so on. In other words, she stresses that, like men, women talk in a range of situations and contexts which have a bearing on how they will speak.

Activity

Look at TV dramas such as *Playing the Field*, *Real Women*, *Daylight Robbery*, *Fat Friends* or any other current series that centres on the lives of a closely-knit group of women. Is gossip an important element of the narrative?

(Note: there is no commentary on this activity.)

Soap opera and gossip

Certain television genres have been associated with gossip. In particular, the so called 'women's genre' of soap opera has been used to validate the notion that gossip is a feature of women's talk rather than men's. However, as Myra Macdonald (1995) points out, gossip in soaps has very important narrative functions. It is used to inform new or part-time viewers of plot developments, and also the character associated with gossip is often used to generate humour. In *Coronation Street*, women, such as Vera Duckworth, fill this role. However, older men, such as the butcher Fred Elliott, qualify as gossips too. As Macdonald says, 'the specific community constructed in soap, isolated from the larger world, is an ideal space for gossip, whatever the gender of its originators'.

Nevertheless, many writers point out that female conversation is central to traditional soaps like *Coronation Street*. Christine Geraghty (1992) has argued for the importance of mother–daughter relationships and female friendships in the genre, which, she says, are emphasised

89

when an episode is dedicated to such relationships. If we examine the mother–daughter relationships between *Coronation Street*'s Audrey and Gail, and Gail and Sarah-Louise, Geraghty's point is made clear because these relationships, which focus on female closeness and the characters' ups and downs in their efforts to maintain solidarity, are crucial to the series. Female friendships are just as important too, and soaps frequently show women talking to one another, especially in moments of drama and crisis.

In the section on audience studies discussed in Unit three the role of female viewers gossiping about soaps between episodes was highlighted as important in a viewer remaining engaged with the series. Women talking about soaps to other women often involves giving advice to the characters – 'I don't think she should go back to Kevin', 'I think she should keep the baby'. As Geraghty points out, 'when popular newspapers asked their agony aunts whether or not Deirdre Barlow in *Coronation Street* should remain with her husband or leave him, they were imitating the kinds of conversations which were taking place all over the country'. Thus the viewer tests out the various scenarios in soap through gossip or talking about the episodes with friends. The BBC recognises this use of soaps in advertisements for *EastEnders*. In these advertisements, various actors from the series try to entice the viewers into watching by offering snippets of 'gossip' about dramatic storylines. The ads end with the actor acknowledging:

> '*EastEnders*, everyone's talking about it.'

However, soap as a form has changed over the decades. Soaps have increasingly incorporated elements from other genres, such as crime series, which are associated with action rather than 'gossip' and with central male characters rather than women.

Activity

Watch an episode of *EastEnders* and an episode of *Coronation Street*. Do you think it is still safe to say with any certainty that soap opera is a 'female' television genre?

(Note: there is no commentary on this activity.)

SUMMARY

This unit has introduced a number of approaches to the study of television and represented talk. It has demonstrated that represented talk has narrative purpose and that scripted conversation differs from real conversation. The unit has also explained the concepts of realism and realist codes and connected these to the language of television.

The issue of gender and represented talk has also been discussed, including the ways in which soap opera has been associated with women's speech, and this has been related to cultural attitudes about language-use and gender.

Discourse and television texts

This unit explains the concept of discourse as it is used in the study of culture and the media, first differentiating that usage from other definitions of the term in language studies.

The unit examines the notions of discourse as language, practice, knowledge and power. These aspects of discourse theory are then applied to television texts and some discourses articulated by television texts are examined.

The term discourse is used in different ways in language studies and in the study of the media. Cultural linguist Mary Talbot explains that the word discourse is used in linguistics to mean several things: stretches of language longer than a sentence, language-use and language interaction (written or spoken). She explains further:

> [T]here is a contrasting use of discourse which is incorporated into critical discourse analysis [an area of language study]. Critical discourse analysts use the term discourse in both the linguistic sense of social interaction in specific situations and in the Foucault sense.
> (*Language and Gender*, 1999: 150)

It is this last 'Foucault' sense of the word 'discourse' that this unit examines. We refer to a 'Foucauldian' definition of discourse because this definition of the word derives from the work of French historian and philosopher, Michel Foucault (1926–1984).

DISCOURSES AS WAYS OF SPEAKING

In examining television, the Foucauldian definition of **discourse** explains for us how language used in television texts connects to a world outside the text. The language of texts therefore connects to wider systems of thought and to social relations.

Very simply, discourse can be thought of as ways of speaking about the world: ways of using language which create ways of understanding the world. This implies also that discourse creates ways of thinking and behaving, which, as we shall see, also relate to social practices and institutions.

To take an example of discourse further, we can say that 'education' is a prominent discourse because it involves a set of ideas and language that provides a particular way of understanding the social world. Such ideas and language have accompanying social practices which involve, for example, appointing teachers, defining subjects to learn and sending children to school. The most widespread example of 'education' in our culture is that of the compulsory education of children and young adults by other adults in the school and college system. British Prime Minister Tony Blair invoked this discourse when, on his election in 1997, he said that his government's priorities were 'Education, education, education'.

This discourse of education employs certain ways of speaking about the world which carry assumptions. Specific language-use within the discourse of education makes the assumption, for example, that to 'be educated' is desirable and necessary, so to be 'uneducated' is usually to be socially deficient in some way.

'Education' – a noun derived from the verb 'to educate' – implies within the school system that it is something which is done to people, a transaction between those who do the educating and those who are educated. Specific names are given to the roles of the educators and the educated, like 'teachers' and 'students'. Education discourse also assumes that the process should be competitive and that some people will be better at being educated; this is evident in examples of language like 'achievement', 'testing', 'grades' and the identification of 'brighter' or 'more able' students.

Activity

Using an example of a television drama featuring school or college life, for instance *Hollyoaks*, *Grange Hill* or *Neighbours*, identify specific examples of language associated with 'education'.

In what ways do these examples construct a particular version of society? For example, what assumptions does this language make about the role of 'education'?

(Note: there is no commentary on this activity.)

UNITY, EXCLUSION AND PRODUCTION

Discourses work on principles of both unification and exclusion. An important characteristic of discourses is that they work to unify particular sets of ideas and beliefs. Discourses are ways of speaking that emphasise the things that bind sets of ideas and practices together, as well as excluding the things that oppose them.

For example, when Britain was fighting the Second World War, its government employed a patriotic discourse of 'Britain' and 'Britishness' in public communications, in order to unify the people of the nation.

Patriotic media propaganda used notions of 'Britain' as an idea rather than a geographical place. Sets of symbols and values were referred to in this particular patriotic discourse. These symbols were a combination of grand notions such as the monarchy and the Shakespearean romance of:

> This royal throne of kings, this scepter'd isle
> [. . .]
> This fortress built by Nature for herself
> Against infection and the hand of war;
> This happy breed of men, this little world;

> This precious stone set in a silver sea,
> [. . .]
> This blessed plot, this earth, this realm, this England.
>
> > (*Richard II*, 2.1)

and also ordinary things like the British Bulldog, the gallant 'Tommy' soldier and cheerful old music hall songs like 'Boiled Beef and Carrots'. It was important to emphasise values of 'ordinariness' because the government needed people from all social and economic classes to think of themselves as fighting for the war effort. For example, those not actually fighting on the various battle fronts, such as mothers and older men, were referred to as fighting on the 'home front'.

The British government controlled all film-making during the war and commissioned films which created positive accounts of the fighting forces. These 'propaganda' films used a discourse of 'Britishness', constructing a notion of the 'British character' that implied that all people in Britain shared 'British' qualities. Characters in the 'forces' films were dogged, fair-minded and brave, but also had homely qualities like a sense of humour. 'Britain' and 'Britishness' were powerful discourses which encouraged people of different social classes and of the different cultures, regions and nations of Britain to believe that they were fighting for a unified set of 'British' values. This is evident in such wartime films as *The Way Ahead* (1944), in which men who have occupied very different social positions in civilian life are conscripted together to fight as a team in an infantry unit, or the 1942 film *In Which We Serve*, which shows the three different families of serving sailors on the same warship, from the working, middle and upper social classes, all united in making a Christmas toast to the ship, a symbol of Britain, as their primary loyalty.

In pre-war Britain there had been much tension over inequalities between economic and social classes. This patriotic discourse therefore attempted to exclude the inevitable conflicts and contradictions of people's lives for the duration of the war.

DOMINANT DISCOURSES

Foucault argued that certain discourses have become dominant as ways of explaining the world and regulating society in Western Europe since the eighteenth century. One of these **dominant discourses** is 'science', which includes medical science and psychiatry, both of which provide explanations about people, their bodies and behaviour.

A scientific discourse may seem to be quite different to, for instance, a political discourse. 'Environmentalism', for example, is perceived as just one set of ideas and beliefs amongst many that provide explanations about the economy and the environment. 'Biology', on the other hand, is thought of as the discovery and impartial study of the natural world, which has a solid, timeless existence.

Foucault challenged the idea that science merely studies 'natural' things. For instance, he argued that it was only during the nineteenth century that 'the homosexual' became regarded by society as a distinct type of person, and that homosexual sex only became criminalised in the Victorian era, when it also became seen as evidence of an abnormal psychology. This does not mean that, previously, people did not have same-sex relationships, nor that society approved of such relations, but it did mean that people were not called 'homosexuals' or 'heterosexuals' or defined primarily by these sexual preferences. Psychiatric science therefore created new language which classified people as essentially 'homosexual' or 'heterosexual' and marked 'the homosexual' as deviant and also as 'ill' in some way. Psychiatry therefore produced discourses – new ways of speaking – about sexuality.

Before the eighteenth century, madness was regarded as a characteristic of wicked, harmless or holy 'fools'. However, madness later came to be seen instead as a disease or disorder, defined by the discourse of medical science. The language therefore changed: holy, wise or immoral 'fools' or 'lunatics' became 'mental patients'.

In both these examples, categories changed because of the new 'knowledge' produced by medical science. These examples indicate that the categories by which people are defined are not timeless and natural but depend on the dominant discourses of the day.

Discourses, then, do not only exclude things but they also actively create 'knowledges' about the world which come to be accepted as natural, impartial or common sense. At any one time, some discourses will be more readily accepted, more dominant, within a society than others. Discourses do not simply reflect the relations between people and groups which power consists of, they help to shape those power relations.

MEDIA DISCOURSES ABOUT AIDS

During the 1980s and 1990s, the British media circulated an increasing number of discourses about HIV (the virus) and AIDS (the disease it causes). Since many of us have little direct experience of HIV or AIDS, our knowledge of them is produced according to these discourses, usually disseminated via the popular mass media.

One strand of reporting, prompted by Government information campaigns, concentrated on the medical discourses of AIDS. This reporting emphasised the notion of the risk of spreading disease and prescribed ways of preventing it. People with HIV/AIDS were constructed as 'patients' and 'victims' of AIDS. It also created the use of the notion of 'high-risk groups', such as gay men and intravenous drug users. There was considerable emphasis in this strand on the dissemination of information about 'responsible' hygienic practices, such as sexual restraint and the use of condoms.

Another strand of reporting used discourses which centred on panic and threat, as John Eldridge records in the book *Message Received* (1999). A phrase which began to be used about AIDS identified the disease as a 'gay plague'. This discourse combines a notion of disease as a sudden threat to the entire community with a religious notion of punishment. In the past, plagues had been seen as divine punishment for peoples' sinfulness.

This notion of sin was reinforced by news reporting referring to 'innocent victims' of AIDS – for example, people who had received contaminated blood transfusions – which implied that others, such as the 'homosexuals, bisexuals and junkies' frequently invoked by the tabloids, were 'guilty'.

This panic discourse combined with other discourses which created notions of threat from outside, usually concerning 'foreigners'. Some tabloids warned, for instance, about the threat to British girls going on holiday abroad and being romanced by Mediterranean Romeos. The speculation that AIDS had originated in Africa and had been brought in to the US by people from Haiti emphasised a mistrust of 'foreigners' and of non-white peoples.

In response to these strands of reporting, organisations representing some groups that had been affected by both AIDS and the media reporting of it began to put together media campaigns which created new discourses around AIDS. For instance, the New York gay rights group Act Up campaigned against the stigmatisation of homosexual sex and lack of funding for drugs to treat the disease with its SILENCE = DEATH slogan. Also at this time, the AIDS quilt campaign publicised the creation of a vast commemorative quilt – a very 'homely' American tradition – for gay men and others who had died of AIDS, emphasising their personalities and identities as sons, lovers, mothers, and so on. More liberal media discourses around AIDS were later marked by examples such as the mainstream Hollywood film *Philadelphia* in 1993.

Examine the language in Text: Breast cancer and Text: Acne, which draw on discourses we could call 'medical science', 'alternative medicine' or 'folk medicine' and 'health and beauty'. Identify how you think the language-use supports these particular discourses. Discuss the implications of these extracts in terms of people's attitudes towards their health.

These texts are both from the 'Health' sections of monthly ('glossy') women's magazines.

Text: Breast cancer

Breast cancer update

Women who carry the high-risk genes for breast cancer known as BRCA 1 and 2 will soon have access to a new breast-screening test. A small amount of fluid is taken from the nipple, then analysed for a biochemical marker that could indicate the presence of cancer. It is hoped that, if a trial of the test is successful, it will become an easier, more effective test than mammography. Women who have such genes account for only five to ten per cent of breast-cancer cases, but if this trial goes well, there will be more trials with lower-risk women. If you have at least four relatives under sixty who have had breast cancer, you may want to consider discussing gene-testing with your GP.

Text: Acne

When your skin breaks out,
is it a clue to hidden health problems?

Do you feel like a grown-up woman with teenage skin? You're not alone, 'Acne is affecting more and more people in their 20s, 30s and 40s', says dermatologist Dr ___. According to Chinese medicine, the cause of adult spots is more than skin deep – and where you get them reveals a lot about your health and lifestyle.

So what do your spots reveal about your health?

1 Upper and lower forehead

Problem organs
Spots on the upper forehead are linked to bladder problems; and on the lower forehead to the intestines.

Lifestyle imbalances
You could be eating too much sugar, milk, juices, red meat, saturated fat and proteins or taking a lot of drugs and medications.

Skin solution
Your body is having trouble eliminating the above foods – cutting down on these should help with detoxification.

2 Between the eyebrows

Problem organ
Liver.

Lifestyle imbalances
You may be eating too much fat, fried foods and dairy products; try cutting down on alcohol, too.

Skin solution
Instead of frying, try grilling or baking food, or stir-fry with olive oil. Also the liver symbolises anger and frustration – suppressing these emotions can lead to an imbalance in liver energy, which eventually shows up as spots. Herbal remedies commonly used in the treatment of liver conditions include Chinese angelica and white peony.

As societies and cultures change over time, so do discourses and, as discourses change, so do the knowledges they create. This happened in Britain after the initial moral panic about AIDS. The dominant media discourses of HIV and AIDS later became fusions of medical and educational discourses about sexual safety, combined with discourses that asserted the social rights of gays, immigrants and young people not to be stigmatised, in addition to the refusal by youth culture to stigmatise drug-use and sexual activity as inherently dangerous.

Extension

Identify different ways in which HIV and HIV+ people, as well as people with AIDS, are represented in current publicity and mass media. You could look at web sites, newspapers or television, or in student information centres.

Can you identify different discourses – ways of speaking – that are being used in your examples?

SUBJECT-POSITIONS

Discourses create subject-positions – roles and identities – for people. The homosexual and the mental patient were new subject-positions created by medical science. Different and complex subject-positions are produced by different discourses: for example, the discourse of medicine produces subject-positions of doctor and patient; law produces those of judges, police officers, jailors and prisoners; and education produces those of teachers and pupils, lecturers and students. However, these subject-positions operate temporarily rather than being completely fixed. When students are in class they will probably accept the role and authority of the lecturer. However, that does not mean that, outside the class, they will still accept that authority, nor will they expect to be lectured in a nightclub.

Some subject-positions carry particular social authority, such as that of a police officer. However, a police officer also simultaneously occupies other subject-positions created within other discourses. For example,

101

within a discourse of 'the family', an officer may well also be a mother, a husband or a son. The subject-positions mentioned so far have different and unequal relationships to others; that is, some subject-positions are more powerful than others.

Importantly, subject-positions created by discourses are generally accepted by people and are internalised to form part of their self-identities. This may be positive in terms of one's sense of self or it may be negative. It may also limit and constrain our sense of who we are, and our different subject-positions may conflict with one another.

Activity

Identify subject-positions you feel you occupy or have occupied in the past, for example within the family. Give examples of the language which describes these subject-positions and the relationships they construct between you and other people.

Commentary

A married woman with young children might be positioned as a mother and regarded in terms of a subject-position that predicts her role and priorities as involvement with domesticity, rather than employment, and so on. This discourse may be a part of her self-identity, but she may have other aspects to her self-identity. She may also be in paid employment outside the home and, therefore, be regarded in terms of a subject-position that predicts characteristics which conflict with her identity of 'mother'.

To the extent that discourses regulate and control our self-images and actions, we are constructed by discourse. Individuals are said to be **subjects** of discourse. In terms of television, one of the ways in which texts use discourse is in the construction and representation of characters, so the consumption of television texts is one of the ways in which audiences are subjected to discourse.

For example, *Buffy the Vampire Slayer* articulates discourses concerning dominant US cultural values. In the series, Buffy's task is to protect America from the vampires who threaten its stability, so her fight with them is also a fight over certain values. In one particular episode, a vampire casts a spell on the adults in Buffy's community that makes them behave irresponsibly. They revert to their youth – they smoke, drink and become sexually promiscuous. In other words, these adults who usually occupy particular subject-positions in discourse, temporarily step out of this position when they flout its rules. This representation relates to the wider social world and discourses about appropriate subject-positions that adults occupy within it. In watching *Buffy*, then, we are subjected to a certain discourse about social morality that assumes and offers us particular ways of thinking, acting and speaking.

Texts set up subject-positions that are structured on an opposition between 'us' and 'them'. For example, in *Buffy* the text privileges Buffy's point of view and invites us to identify with her as the protector of society. In contrast, the vampires are constructed so that we feel little empathy with them and the text encourages us to regard them as a threat.

To use another example, news reporting is structured towards the perspective of 'us', who are positioned as the holders of certain values and judgements that are given privilege; this subject-position is then contrasted with 'them' who are seen to hold a different set of values.

This happens in news reporting when teenage pregnancy is talked about in relation to social problems such as poverty and crime. The discourse of the text reproduces certain attitudes towards women, but it has the appearance of neutrality and the status of truth.

Activity

Watch or videotape a television news broadcast or a drama. Identify a range of subject-positions that the text constructs. What kinds of social judgements and values are attached to these representations?

(Note: there is no commentary on this activity.)

DISCOURSES OF GENDER AND SEXUALITY ON TV: SOME EXAMPLES

There are no discourses specific to television that cannot be referred to the wider world. However, television texts will use different discourses in various ways. The following are examples of how particular discourses may be articulated – used as ways of speaking – by popular television genres.

Documentary films may articulate discourses of science and nature, making use of the status of these discourses as dealing with 'facts' about the world. Sports quiz programmes articulate discourses about masculinity in their 'laddish' exchanges and not altogether serious hero-worship of certain male sports figures. Generic television drama, whether police, historical or soap opera, may articulate a whole range of social discourses about gender, age, ethnicity, regionality, social class and sexuality. Television comedy, on the other hand, from sitcom to stand-up, often seeks to spoil the effect of 'serious' discourses, such as when satirical impressionist Rory Bremner mocks the discourse of politics by portraying the Prime Minister as a holier-than-thou vicar and other politicians as self-serving and hypocritical.

The concept of discourse, then, emphasises the power of ideas and ways of thinking about topics that have the status of truth and knowledge. Discourse is also important because it provides us with a language for talking about television texts that relate them to particular historical moments. For example, if we examine the way in which teen pregnancy was talked about in a 1980s episode of *EastEnders* and then compare that text with an episode from the year 2000, we would find that particular discourse about the issue has altered over a decade or so.

In our culture there are discourses about teenage pregnancy which are not only evident in soaps. These discourses are disseminated from different sites such as medicine, religions, government and politics, and they reappear in media artefacts such as films, pop songs and television programmes. These discourses together define what it is possible to say about this issue. For example, our knowledge of the issue and the ways in which the existence of teen pregnancies has come to be regarded as a poor state of affairs has been regulated by discourses or statements about the topic.

Our knowledge has also been constituted, at least in part, by the ways in which the media construct types of girls who in certain ways symbolise the discourse. An example would be the inappropriately sexually active fifteen-year-old in television drama who represents the characteristics we would expect of a potential teen mum, since this is the way our knowledge about the issue has been constructed. We also need to be aware of the ways in which our knowledge of the issue has the status of truth through the mediation of discourse in, for example, a news bulletin, which assumes that single motherhood is the cause of rising crime and poverty in Britain.

Ally McBeal

The concept of discourse can be usefully applied to focus on privileged representations of women. For example, the television series *Ally McBeal* can be studied as a text that reproduces discourses circulating in the real world that have produced knowledge about women's role in society. In the series, Ally McBeal is a single, professional woman who is anxious because she longs for the things that the more traditional woman seems to have – a happy marriage and children. She is always looking back to a golden era at university when she was in love with Billy, whom she rejected after graduating when she started working as a lawyer because she misguidedly chose her career over personal relationships. Ally has lived to regret that decision because professional success has not fulfilled her and much of the programme is concerned with Ally's yearning for romance and motherhood.

This prominent discourse in *Ally McBeal* relates to our discursive knowledge about women's roles today. Discourses ranging from sexual politics to the law, which have the status of truth about women, have produced ways of talking about women's progress in achieving equality with men over the last few decades. This discourse tells us that women's struggles for equality have been successful, but at a price. In women's magazines, films, self-help books, popular fiction and psychology books, women, like Ally, are not happy and are likely to be suffering from stress and a deep sense of unfulfilled needs. Since the 1980s, the media have also produced language to talk about this condition, for example the terms 'man shortage' and 'biological clock'.

This discourse is also evident in visual images. Certain visual codes through which this particular discourse of femininity is signified can also be identified if we focus on Ally's appearance. Ally's image is not an isolated or unique version of femininity – it appears across a range of sites from advertising to music videos and Hollywood film. She is in her late twenties and has emphatic facial features: big eyes, full lips and prominent cheekbones. She wears a broad-shouldered business suit connotative of masculinity, but the way in which it hangs from her waif-like body produces an image associated with the career woman that is a combination of both masculine and feminine elements, of both strength and weakness.

105

What these images refer to is an assertive masculinity that Ally adopts, which attempts, but without success, to conceal the 'real' Ally who is connotative of childlike femininity; thus, the visual images produce an image of Ally as someone who is self-absorbed and desperately unhappy.

Activity

Examine images of men and/or women in a popular 'glossy' magazine such as *New Woman* or *FHM,* and try to identify how these relate to your existing knowledge about masculinity and/or femininity.

Examine the main characters in such dramas as *Sex in the City* or *Queer as Folk,* and try to identify the ways in which their lifestyles – their professional status, social lives, preoccupations, possessions and so on – relate to discourses about gender and sexuality.

(Note: there is no commentary on this activity.)

Coronation Street **and** *EastEnders*

It is important to be aware that dominant discourses can be replaced. For example, in the eighteenth century certain discourses about gender produced 'knowledges' about men's supposed rationality and superior intelligence over women's supposed irrationality and comparative lack of intelligence. However, these discourses have since been challenged by **feminist** discourses, especially feminist scientific discourses. Foucault stressed that the truth status of discourse is open to critique and that there are oppositional discourses emanating from certain spheres. This means that the ways in which discourse can adapt or change can be accounted for.

For example, a dominant Western discourse, referred to as 'patriarchy' ('rule by the father'), which constructed privileged social roles for men and subordinate roles for women, has been adapting itself since the 1970s, when a new and increasingly authoritative feminist discourse threatened its dominance. One of the ways in which patriarchy incorporated some of the elements of feminist discourse was that it changed from a discourse that attempted to justify women's confinement in the home as housewives and mothers to one that is more tolerant of women's own needs, such as wanting to have careers. So new representations of working women have emerged in all aspects of the media including magazines, advertising, television and film.

Another important way of thinking about discourse and texts is to recognise that a text has more than one 'voice' because different discourses are always interacting and entering into arguments within them. We could, for example, see these competing discourses in a television text such as a soap, played out in narrative, characters, languages and images.

The year 2000 saw an interesting development in the discourse regarding teenage pregnancy. Two soaps, *EastEnders* and *Coronation Street*, ran major storylines on the issue and both, in certain ways, privileged a certain discourse that contradicted dominant discourses about schoolgirl pregnancy. The characters, Sonia and Sarah-Louise, did not personify the dominant discourse of the knowing, 'bad', sexually-aware teenager. Instead the characters were given attributes we do not expect these people to have.

Below is a list of the attributes we often associate with such teenage girls, and another list of the attributes of Sonia and Sarah-Louise.

'THEM'	SONIA and SARAH-LOUISE
mature	childlike
aggressive	unsure
sexually mature	sexually naïve
knowing	innocent
irresponsible	responsible
lazy	hardworking
bad	good

However, this does not mean that the text is monolithic or only has this one discourse. Other discourses are in dialogue with one another throughout the text. In *Coronation Street*, for example, the moralising, judgemental discourse that blames teenage pregnancy for all that threatens the stability of society, is articulated through the character of Blanche, a conservative, moralising older woman. She connects teen pregnancy with a supposed breakdown of 'family life' and therefore of the social order. However, Hayley, who is a male-to-female transsexual, expressed a different discourse about compassion and tolerance of peoples' varying life circumstances; she felt sympathy towards Sarah as a young girl in trouble and offered practical help and support.

On the other hand, Sarah's mother Gail articulated yet another discourse about parenting and maternal responsibility in regard to the issue of teenage girls' emerging sexuality in the context of the family. Gail took much of the responsibility for the unplanned pregnancy and agonised over her possible failures as a mother, feeling that there had been a breakdown of communication between her and her daughter. Educational and medical discourses about the issue were also present in scenes set within Sarah's school, the hospital, and with her GP and social worker at the point where it had to be decided how Sarah's pregnancy would affect her schooling and what health care and social support she and her baby should have.

At different times and in different contexts all these discourses were in dialogue with each other when characters talked to one another and gave their opinions about Sarah's pregnancy.

Activity

Watch an episode of any popular soap and examine the different discourses which interact with one another over a particular issue. Possible issues are:

- crime
- sexuality
- generation differences
- the family
- motherhood, fatherhood and other male and female roles
- ethnicity/'race'.

(Note: there is no commentary on this activity.)

SUMMARY

This unit has explained relevant aspects of Foucauldian discourse theory, identifying a definition of discourse as a 'way of speaking' about the world, and has connected this to social practices, institutions, identities and values.

The unit has also demonstrated how discourses are apparent in television texts, giving specific examples of discourses about gender and sexuality articulated by particular television programmes.

further reading

Coates, J. (1986) *Women, Men and Language: A sociolinguistic account of sex differences in language*, Harlow: Longman.

Crisell, A. (1999) 'Broadcasting: Television and radio' in J. Stokes and A. Reading (eds) *The Media in Britain*, Basingstoke: Macmillan.

Eldridge, J. (1999) 'Risk, Society and the Media: Now you see it now you don't' in G. Philo (ed.) *Message Received*, Harlow: Longman.

Faludi, S. (1992) *Backlash: The undeclared war against women*, London: Chatto & Windus.

Fiske, J. and Hartley, J. (1978) *Reading television*, London: Methuen.

Geraghty, C. (1992) 'A Woman's Space: Women and soap opera' in F. Bonner, L. Goodman, R. Allen, L. Janes and K. King (eds) *Imagining Women*, Cambridge: Polity Press.

Gledhill, C. (1992) 'Pleasurable negotiations' in F. Bonner, L. Goodman, R. Allen, L. Janes and K. King (eds) *Imagining Women*, Cambridge: Polity Press.

Gledhill, C. (1997) 'Genre and Gender: The case of soap opera' in S. Hall (ed.) *Representation*, London: Sage Publications Ltd.

Hall, S. (1980) 'Encoding/decoding' in S. Hall et al. (eds) *Culture, Media, Language*, London: Hutchinson.

Hall, S. (1997) (ed.) *Representation*, London: Sage Publications Ltd.

Hobson, D. (1982) *Crossroads: The drama of a soap opera*, London: Methuen.

Jones, M. and Jones, E. (1999) *Mass Media*, London: Palgrave.

Macdonald, M. (1995) 'Voices Off: Women, discourse and the media' in *Representing Women*, London: Edward Arnold.

Morley, D. (1986) *Family Television: Cultural power and domestic leisure*, London: Comedia.

Nixon, S. (1997) 'Exhibiting Masculinity' in S. Hall (ed.) *Representation*, London: Sage Publications Ltd.

O'Sullivan, T., Dutton, B. and Rayner, P. (eds) (1998) *Studying the Media* (2nd edn), London and New York: Edward Arnold.

Talbot, M. (1999) *An Introduction to Language and Gender*, Oxford: Blackwell.

Thompson, J.B. (1995) *The Media and Modernity: A social theory of the media*, London: Polity Press.

Wardhaugh, R. (1985) *How Conversation Works*, Oxford: Blackwell.

Wardhaugh, R. (1992) *An Introduction to Sociolinguistics*, Oxford: Blackwell.

Williams, R. (1990) *Television: Technology and cultural form* (2nd edn, ed. Ederyn Williams), London: Routledge.

index of terms

accent 73

The distinctive sounds of the speech of a particular region. Also associated with social class in Britain, in that the prestigious accent Received Pronunciation is traditionally spoken by members of the upper social classes. Such speakers are sometimes mistakenly referred to as having 'no accent'.

agendas 67

Defined here in the context of cooperative conversation to mean that the various participants have their own set of, possibly incompatible, aims and objectives that they wish to achieve in the course of the conversation and towards which they will attempt to steer the conversation.

audience 4

Although often used generally to refer to a group or mass of tele-vision/film viewers as distinct from 'readers' of written works, the term is used in media and cultural studies to refer to those who read and interpret any specific text regardless of its form.

backtracking 81

When investigating features of language use, it refers to the non-fluency of speech which results in the need for self-correction or repetition.

cohesion 68

Refers to the rules governing conversation, prose, narrative, etc., which make them understandable as a whole, so that readers may infer that elements of the conversation or narrative cohere or refer to one another meaningfully. For example, in these sentences:

I saw my Dad in town the other day. He didn't see me, though.

we know by convention that the pronoun 'he' in the following sentence refers back to 'my Dad' of the previous sentence. In a soap opera, for example, we know by convention that the final shot of a woman looking shocked on discovering her husband talking to another woman refers back to the introduction of the character of the other woman as being her husband's ex-wife, something we may need to know for the scene to be meaningful.

common ground 66

Refers to the shared assumptions which participants in cooperative conversation have already established or will seek to establish.

connotation/denotation 30

Denotation is a sign's literal or directly conceptual meaning. A chair is the object we name as a

111

chair or a description of it in its most functional aspect as something we sit on.

Connotations are the secondary meanings produced through associations with a sign. For example, a chair can suggest a wealthy lifestyle, nostalgia, comfort, functionality, youth and so on. An armchair that looks old might generate connotations of tradition, safety and so on. On the other hand, if made of chrome it might suggest youth and modernity.

consumption 4
The process or act of engaging with and responding to media texts.

correctness 74
The assumption that there is a correct English which is superior to regional accents and dialects. However, the idea that any English dialect can be judged to be inferior to any other is disputed by linguists who argue that all English dialects are equally complex and valid language systems.

cultural realism 85
The ways in which a text refers to beliefs and values held in the wider social world.

culture 4
Can be defined in different ways and is often used to refer to the intellectual or artistic products of a society, but here it is used to mean the various lived experiences and ways of life of a society and of groups within that society, including its popular creative products such as television.

decoding 56
The process of reading or interpreting a text. (See also **encoding**)

denotation 30
(see **connotation**)

dialect 73
The distinctive lexis and syntax of the language variety – English, for example, has many varieties – of a particular region. Also associated with social class in Britain, in that Standard English, the form which is reproduced in dictionaries and grammars, tends to also be the home dialect of the upper social classes.

direct address 64
One of the main features of live television is the presence of a person (or persons) speaking directly to camera and therefore to the audience. For example, evening news broadcasts usually feature a newsreader who delivers their scripted commentary via either close-ups or medium shots with little camera movement and virtually no cuts unless to go over to another reporter.

discourse 94
Language as groups of statements comprised of rules and conventions that convey ways of thinking about the world. At any given moment there will be authoritative **dominant discourses**, which produce knowledge about the world and govern the way the world is talked about, when, where and by whom. At the same time, there are alternative or **subordinate discourses** that compete with these. Thus, in the Western world

there is a particular dominant discourse about medicine, which governs the way illness and treatment are talked about, but there is also a subordinate discourse emanating in the field of homoeopathy which competes with this.

disequilibrium 50

The lack of balance, harmony or normality produced by dramatic events that trigger the action in a text. This state of affairs can be caused by an enigma, quest, misunderstandings between characters and so on.

dominant discourse 96
(see **discourse**)

dominant reading 56

The first of three main kinds of readings or decodings of television texts proposed by Hall (1980). The dominant reading interprets the text according to the assumptions of the encoder. Let us consider, for example, an advertisement for washing powder that depicts a woman who seems to delight in looking after her family. A dominant reading would accept this representation as natural, normal and desirable. **Negotiated reading** is the second kind of reading or decoding of texts and acknowledges the authority of the dominant code, but responds by adapting the reading according to the specific social position of the decoder. An example of a negotiated reading would be for a female student to accept the preferred reading – 'my mum's like that and I'm pleased that she is' – while thinking 'there is no way I could ever do it'. Finally, **oppositional reading** is the third

of the main possible readings and produces a decoding that is radically opposed to the preferred reading. An oppositional reading may be produced by the student if, say, she is a feminist. She may read the advertisement as a sign of women's continued subordination in society.

effects model 4

Seen now as highly problematic, this model is no longer utilised as a means of talking about audiences. However, initially, audiences were assumed by producers, advertisers and researchers to be a predictable, undifferentiated mass who responded to media texts in a uniform way.

encoding 56

The process of constructing a text by means of visual and aural language, which are combined according to certain conventions. The perceptions of the encoder and decoder are crucial in television's production–text– audience circle, so cultural beliefs, values and experiences are factors that are emphasised at each stage. (See also **decoding**)

equilibrium 50

When applied to texts it refers to the state of balance, normality or harmony that often exists at the beginning and end of a narrative.

feedback 82

When analysing features of language-use it is a term that covers all examples of responses to speakers. The intention of feedback can be to signal agreement, support and encouragement, or it may signal boredom, disagreement, and so on.

113

feminist 106

One who holds the view that females, within certain cultures, are unequal or subordinate in relation to men. Feminist criticism is the analysis of individual texts or the processes of their production and consumption from a feminist perspective.

fictional realism 85

The ways in which a text relates to the conventions and rules of the fictional world. For example, science fiction has its own distinct rules regarding realism, which means that a text can be set in a futuristic world even though we know this is not possible in the real world.

genre 39

A type of text. There are particular and recognisable characteristics that exist within a text that relate it to other texts. Individual television texts are recognised as belonging to a particular genre – the soap opera, sitcom, and documentary are three examples of television genres.

gossip 88

Generally it refers to women's use of language but, when used in media and cultural studies, it refers to the ways in which women use language to construct a female discourse and culture that is distinct from men's.

hesitation markers 81

When investigating features of language in use they refer to a wide variety of sounds that fill the gaps that are needed to give a speaker time for thought.

horizontal 4

The various programmes that are broadcast at the same time across all available television stations.

hybrid 47

A combination of two or more original elements. A text that is produced through fusing the conventions of two or more other genres. Docu-soaps are texts that combine elements of documentary with elements of soap opera.

iconicity 19

The extent to which a signifier physically resembles its signified. A photograph of Tony Blair is more iconic than a portrait of him. A portrait may be more iconic than a cartoon drawing of him.

interjection 81

The term covers all examples of short overlaps in speech that do not interrupt the flow of the main speaker.

interrupting 81

When a new speaker begins their turn, which prevents the previous speaker finishing theirs.

intertextuality 47

The way in which texts interconnect and interact with one another. The American animated sitcom, *The Simpsons*, frequently refers to other texts such as television programmes (*Itchy and Scratchy* is a reference to the cartoon tradition of *Tom and Jerry*), pop music and film.

linear 50

In media and cultural studies this term refers to the classic structure of narrative that presents the telling of a story in chronological order. Sometimes narrative is non-linear. For example, the film *Pulp Fiction* presents events in non-chronological order which means that viewers have to work out for themselves the time and space in which events are happening.

mediating 63
The act of relaying and interpreting the wider culture to those who do not have direct experience of it.

metaphor 32
When a word or visual sign works by transporting qualities from one plane of reality to another, e.g. 'John always comes up smelling of roses'.

metonym 34
When an image or word which is an attribute or part of something stands in for or represents the whole. e.g. 'Jill is on the stage' (is part of the acting profession). Similarly, a journalist's photograph of a young man sleeping in a shop doorway represents the issue of homelessness.

minimal responses 81
Special kinds of interjection that are supportive and cooperative.

mise en scène 84
The French term for the visual arrangement of a scene or set. It includes scenery, costume, lighting and camera angles, as well as actors' movements, such as a woman washing dishes or a man reading a newspaper.

mode of address 64
The method or way in which a television text addresses us.

monological 3
Television communication is a one-way process in the sense that a single text sends messages to a mass audience who cannot interact with it in the same way that they can in, for example, a telephone conversation.

narrative 24
The organising or structuring of a story according to certain conventions and devices that can be formally identified. Narrative involves the recounting of an event or events and these can be either real or fictitious. The person telling their life story to a chat-show host is delivering a narrative in the same way that Bridget does in *Bridget Jones's Diary*.

negotiated reading 57
(see **dominant reading**)

new equilibrium 50
When applied to texts it refers to the new state of balance or harmony that often exists at the end of a narrative.

oppositional reading 57
(see **dominant reading**)

ownership 3
The media industry is a huge money-making enterprise which has implications for its role in society. For example, in some countries television stations are owned and controlled by the state, whereas in other countries television stations are owned and controlled by media moguls. In media and cultural studies, it is

perceived that a full understanding of a text must involve
studying it from this aspect as
well as carrying out textual
analysis and audience studies.

paradigms 22
(see **syntagms**)

phatic 68
Phatic talk fulfils a primarily social
role, creating ease and
commonality between people.
Remarks made to a neighbour
or colleague about the weather,
such as 'Gosh, it's hot isn't it?',
to which they reply 'Yes, I'm
boiling!', are redundant in terms
of information given (both
participants already know that it
is hot) but are a way of marking
ongoing friendly relations between
the two.

polysemy 55
The capacity of all texts to
generate multiple meanings rather
than conveying a single, fixed
meaning.

preferred 56
A text is open to more than one
reading but the aim of analysing
it is sometimes to reveal its
'preferred' or dominant one.

production 3
Refers to the ways in which
texts are made and draws
attention to the fact that the
media is potentially a powerful
agent of cultural beliefs and
values. In television news, for
example, it refers to the process
of news production, such as
selection processes, involved in
the production of news
broadcasts.

read 26
To perform the act of
comprehending and interpreting
the meaning of a text.

realism 83
An umbrella term that refers to
the strategies and devices that are
used in the making of texts in
order to enable a text to offer an
appearance or an illusion of the
real world.

realist codes 84
Particular conventions or systems
of meaning used by members of a
culture or subculture. A code
consists of signs – words or images
– and the rules that govern how
they can be used.

scheduling 4
The way in which television
programmes are time-tabled with
the aim of gaining the largest
audience possible.

semiotics 15
The study of signs and sign
systems and how they generate
meaning within certain social
contexts.

signified 18
(see **signs**)

signifier 18
(see **signs**)

signify 16
(see **sign system**)

signs 15
A sign has three characteristics –
a physical form; that to which it
refers; and the ability to be
recognised by people as a sign.
A sign is comprised of two
elements – the signifier or physical

form; and the signified or the mental concept of what it refers to.

sign system 15
Signs work together in systems. The way traffic lights work is an example of a simple sign system. Red is used to **signify** 'stop', and green to signify 'go'.

situational variation 64
Refers to the changes in language use which occur in different situations or according to which roles are being played. We use various levels of politeness and formality depending on who we are talking to, or we use different language in fulfilling different roles, such as being a customer in a pub, a lawyer presenting a case or a student having a tutorial.

subjects 102
The term draws attention to the individual as being subjected to a complexity of social factors. Thus identity or sense of self is not something we are born with, but something we construct in relation to the social world we inhabit.

subordinate discourse (see **discourse**)

symbolic 16
A sign sometimes stands in for something other than itself. The Union Jack represents feelings of national unity, as when, for example, it was flown at half mast at the time of Princess Diana's death.

syntagms 22
Meaningful combinations of signifiers selected from **paradigms**

of available signifiers, such as sentences made of words selected from the paradigm of words available in the English language.

text 3
A specific, chosen work that is to be analysed in terms of its words, images and sounds. Some texts incorporate all these features, for example film and television texts, while others, such as photographs, paperback fiction and magazines, are texts that do not feature sound.

turn-taking 67
The cooperative feature of conversation whereby we allow each participant, to a greater or lesser extent, to make a contribution. Turn-taking is often regulated by verbal cues: if we ask a question, we expect another person to take a turn to speak and to answer it. By asking the question of a particular participant, we have nominated them to speak.

uses and gratifications 4
The view that media audiences use what the media have to offer to satisfy certain needs. According to the researcher Denis McQuail there are four types of need which the media serve to gratify: diversion (emotional release); personal relationships (companionship); personal identity (value reinforcement); surveillance (need for information about the world).

vertical 4
The programmes scheduled over a twenty-four-hour period that have been broadcast on individual television stations.